THE TIGER'S REVENGE

THE STORY OF A LARGELY UNKNOWN AND MOST DARING RAID OF WORLD WAR TWO

BY

EVAN MORRIS

Grosvenor House
Publishing Limited

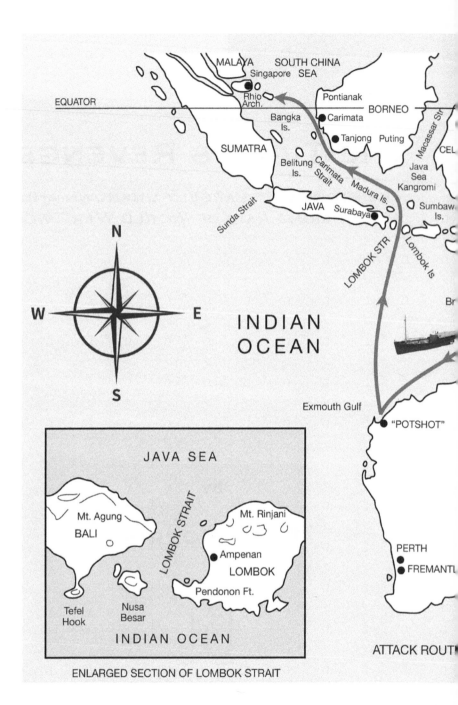

ENLARGED SECTION OF LOMBOK STRAIT

The right of Evan Morris to be identified as the author of this
work has been asserted in accordance with Section 78
of the Copyright, Designs and Patents Act 1988

This book is published by
Grosvenor House Publishing Ltd
Link House
140 The Broadway, Tolworth, Surrey, KT6 7HT.
www.grosvenorhousepublishing.co.uk

A CIP record for this book
is available from the British Library

Paperback ISBN 978-1-80381-593-0
Hardback ISBN 978-1-80381-420-9
eBook ISBN 978-1-80381-421-6

Dedication

I dedicate this book to Jackie, Mark, and Ryan, and thank them for their support, encouragement, and for always being there.

Acknowledgements

My thanks to Lynette Ramsay Silver for assisting with the final edit. Lynette is perhaps the most authoritative source of knowledge relating to both Operation Jaywick and Rimau. Thank you for your considerable contribution.

The Australian War Memorial for supplying high quality photographs relating to Operation Jaywick.

Melanie Bartle, Publishing Administrator at Grosvenor House Publishing for her guidance, encouragement and forbearing.

All proceeds from this book, including royalties, will be donated annually to support ex-service men and women.

Preface

Ronald Morris was not a typical British army soldier. A Welsh man from the Rhonda mining region of South Wales he chose, after five long years as a miner, to join the army and not to stay in the coal mines, in what would become, once war broke out, a reserved occupation. In 1938, a year before the declaration of war against Germany, the young 19-year-old signed up for some adventure. Altruistic by nature, he joined the Royal Army Medical Corps, swapping the valleys of South Wales for the far reaches of the orient in Singapore.

When Japan entered the war, he was recruited to join Special Operations Executive, Orient Mission, and it was at the Headquarters of SOE Orient's 101 Special Training School in Singapore that he met fellow SOE operative, Ivan Lyon. The pair were part of an unorthodox group undertaking clandestine missions and training local 'stay behind teams' to carry out acts of sabotage which were to be undertaken in the event of a British and allied defeat in the defence of Singapore. They also helped establish an escape route through Sumatra, should the Japanese succeed in taking Singapore.

Ronald Morris was my father and was one of a handpicked cadre of men who, following the fall of Singapore, exacted revenge by attacking enemy shipping in Singapore Harbour, on a mission known as Operation Jaywick, led by Ivan Lyon. He and my father became close colleagues while helping hundreds of people escape from Singapore. This shared experience created a deep trust and camaraderie between the two men.

My father was the only person to survive the war who was with Lyon from the escape from Singapore and the inception of

Operation Jaywick. The narrative of this book has been largely reconstructed from wartime documents and the many conversations he and I had over the years. It is through the experiences he shared that I have been able to tell this story of the tumultuous events of that time.

My father as the only UK based serviceman and survivor of Jaywick was interviewed at length for a range of books which were published recording Singapores invasion, its surrender, planning of the escape routes, SOE Orient Mission activities in Singapore and mainland Malaya and of course Operation Jaywick (See bibliography). Individual authors recorded that he was a highly credible witness, who had a descriptive mind and a retentive memory. Books published following his death in 1999 contained some new revelations. Whilst I have used these books in my research I have not included some later accounts or revelations. The Tiger's Revenge is written through the eyes of my father who was either unaware of some events relating to Operation Jaywick or did not disclose them. *The Tigers Revenge* is an honest account which does not seek to embellish the extraordinary mission or anyone involved.

Operation Jaywick was the most successful Special Forces' seaborne raid behind enemy lines in WW2. To this day, it remains a largely unknown event in the annals of military history. Without wishing to diminish the courage and bravery of those involved in Operation Frankton, the 'Cockleshell Heroes', Jaywick was a far greater military success, judged by some to be logistically nearly impossible to succeed, given the distance travelled into deeply guarded and occupied territory.

The Tiger's Revenge will, I hope, allow the reader to grasp the magnitude of what was achieved on this mission from a very personal and unique perspective.

Evan Morris MBE
April 2023

Chapter One

Singapore, Victim of Delusion

Who could have believed that, back in the early 1940s, the British outpost of Singapore and adjoining mainland Malaya with its vast mineral wealth would be the scene of the biggest military humiliation of British history? Fortress Singapore was given the title 'The Gibraltar of the East' by Winston Churchill, such was its strategic importance, and yet all of the natural resources were about to fall into the hands of the Japanese. Great Britain, already at war with Germany and Italy, was heavily embroiled in Europe and North Africa. However, inhabitants of her far-flung strategic stronghold in Singapore were totally unaffected by the horrors of Blitzkrieg and the nightly bombing of London and key major British cities, where 43,500 civilians had been killed and 87,000 seriously injured.

Life in Singapore remained a colonial somnolence, where British expatriates continued to enjoy a lifestyle of privilege that had been taken for granted by the Empire's elite for generations. Even though they accounted for a very small number of the population, they were cosseted and pampered, their every wish attended to by legions of servants, indulging themselves in a way of life that many outside the far east had never known of, let alone experienced. Protected from the reality of the real world, they believed their Nirvana would last forever.

However, the world was becoming a rapidly changing place, something appreciated by enlightened individuals, whose warnings were ignored by both the local population and those who could have done more to prepare for a war that resulted in a great loss of life and humiliating capitulation. At the time, the story of the Japanese onslaught into Malaya, by what the incompetent establishment believed was an inferior race, was a mix of denial, political guile, and deception. We now understand that what happened was almost inevitable, given the tectonic geo-political shifts of that period.

There were those who were sufficiently experienced to know what the outcome would be and were actively working for that eventuality. In London, senior military leaders who advised the Government also realised the futility of the situation. However, either through ignorance or denial, they allowed life to carry on in Singapore until the train hit the proverbial buffers, resulting in humiliation for Britain, mass panic, and the death of many thousands of soldiers, sailors, airmen, men, women and children. This period could easily be labelled 'The betrayal of Singapore'.

In the darkest days of the war, Winston Churchill was confronted with evidence that would shake the foundations of the British Empire's war effort. Eighteen months before the ignominious fall of Singapore, he received evidence that this supposedly heavily defended bastion was, in fact, indefensible. Air Marshall Sir Cyril Newell, Admiral Sir Dudley Pound and General Sir John Dill produced a report, destined for the War Cabinet, containing 87 explosive and detailed paragraphs setting out the vulnerability and ultimate indefensibility of Singapore. The report, seen by senior politicians and the military on 5 August 1940, was considered to be so damning that Winston Churchill decided not to tell the Australian or New Zealand governments.

Churchill was still haunted by the Dardanelles when, as First Sea Lord of the Admiralty in World War I, he was blamed for the loss of thousands of Australian, New Zealand, French and British troops. Slaughtered by machine-gun fire in what was deemed to be a suicide mission. As a result, he could perhaps see the whole event unfolding once again before his very eyes. Churchill did, however, decide in great secrecy to send a copy of the report to Air Chief

Marshall Sir Robert Brooke-Popham, Commander-in-Chief Far East, at his Singapore headquarters. Officials arranged for a courier – the Blue Funnel steamer, *Automedon*, which sailed from Liverpool in September 1940. The Master of the vessel deposited a green canvas bag, marked 'Foreign Office Top Secret', in his safe for secure delivery to military chiefs in Singapore.

On the morning of 11 November, the German surface raider *Atlantis* intercepted *Automedon* in the Indian Ocean – 400 kilometres north-west of Sumatra and close to its destination of Singapore. After *Atlantis* fired off four shells, which hit the bridge and killed the Captain and other crew, a boarding party, captained by Captain Benhard Rogge, recovered the top secret report from the chart room adjoining the bridge, its bag perforated with holes so that it would sink when thrown overboard, a plan that failed to eventuate with the death of the captain. Immediately recognising the report's importance, Rogge sent it without delay to Japan, where it arrived in Kobe on 4 December. The bag was then delivered to Admiral Paul Wenneker, the German Naval attaché in Tokyo. He immediately sent a four-page cipher telegram to his headquarters in Berlin, which was quickly shown to Hitler, who scrawled, 'This is of the utmost importance.'

When Wenneker was ordered to show all of the captured materials to Japanese officials, naval staff realised that they need no longer be concerned about resistance from British and Allied Forces, as their own report showed them to be weak and accepting that the loss of Singapore was inevitable. The report also concluded that the British would respond with little more than diplomatic protest if the Japanese were to encroach on Indochina. The *Automedon* Incident would become known as one of the worst intelligence disasters in history.

As a reward for this intelligence coup, Captain Rogge was awarded with the prestigious Japanese Katana sword, one of only three conferred on Germans. The other two were presented to Reichsmarschall Hermann Goring, and Field Marshall Erwin Rommel.

This information, along with their plan to attack Pearl Harbour, greatly strengthened the resolve and confidence of the Japanese in their quest to expand their Asian Empire. On 30 December 1940, naval intelligence in Singapore told the Admiralty in London that a survivor of *Automedon* had been interviewed by MI6 agents in Tokyo and reported that the Germans had seized the mail on board the vessel. MI6 concluded that, without doubt, the report would have fallen into Japanese hands. Typically, Churchill decided that this information was so sensitive that no one was to know about it. British War Cabinet records made no mention of its loss. Not even Brook-Popham, for whom the report was intended, was informed.

Two days after Pearl Harbour, on 10 December 1941 (Singapore time), two major warships – *Prince of Wales*, the pride of the British fleet, along with *Repulse* – were attacked and sunk in the Gulf of Siam, with a loss of 840 lives. They had been dispatched from Singapore to intercept the Japanese invasion of Thailand, which would prepare the way for the southward onslaught by the Japanese army through Malaya and into Singapore. The ships, operating without air cover, were sunk by torpedoes launched from Japanese bombers. Their original orders, to proceed and protect Singapore, included air cover provided by the aircraft carrier HMS *Indomitable,* but it had run aground on a sandbar in the West Indies, leaving the vessels without fighter protection and aerial reconnaissance.

Troops continued to pour into Singapore from the United Kingdom, Australia, New Zealand and India, right up until the surrender of Singapore on 15 February 1942, when 67,000 Japanese troops of the 25th Army and Imperial Guard captured the fortress and its 140,000 British and Commonwealth forces. Historical research has shown that, if Winston Churchill had made it known that Singapore was indefensible, Australian Prime Minister John Curtin would have withdrawn his troops for the defence of Australia, which at that time was under severe threat.

In 1941, while the high command in Singapore carried on with business as usual, others were preparing for the inevitable – an intelligence network whose members were aware that Singapore had been infiltrated by Japanese spies, supplying a constant flow of intelligence to Tokyo.

In 1940, Special Operations Executive (SOE), which soon became known as 'Churchill's Secret Army' or the 'Ministry of Ungentlemanly Warfare', had been set up in London. In Singapore in 1941, following the incursion of the Japanese military into Southeast Asia, SOE established SOE Far East, known as the Oriental Mission, and set up 101 Special Training School (101 STS) at Tanjung Bali, on the mouth of Singapore's Jurong River. The school was housed in a large, art-deco style bungalow, formerly a millionaire's private estate. The STS brief was to establish stay-behind teams to undertake sabotage and develop resistance groups behind enemy lines in Malaya, to carry on the fight once the British left. The school was training a large number of Chinese Malays, who were mainly Communists and had a natural hatred for the Japanese, due to the long running Sino-Japanese war. So good was their training and preparation that they would later form the nucleus of the highly effective Malayan People's Anti-Japanese Army.

Singapore had a coastline perimeter of 72 miles and had been prepared with defences designed to counter a seaborne invasion, something considered by military chiefs, including Singapore's General Officer Commanding, Arthur Percival, to be highly unlikely. If he and his contemporaries really believed an invasion from the sea was improbable, and that the Malayan jungle made the chances of an invasion from the north almost impossible, their confidence in Singapore's invincibility is understandable. It would not be for the first time in the British Empire's history that such hubris would result in catastrophic loss.

A common misconception was that Singapore's guns pointed out to sea on a fixed line. In fact, all five 15-inch guns could be traversed through 360 degrees. The nine-inch guns sited on Sentosa Island, as well as two six-inch guns, also had full arcs of fire. The problem was that the shells provided were armour piercing, designed to penetrate warships, not high explosive shells used for land-based bombardment.

The systemic belief that the threat to Singapore was from the sea dates back to World War I. The assumption was that the enemy would mount a seaborne attack on the colony's southern shores, rather than a land-based assault on Malaya, into impregnable jungle. British policy for the defence of Singapore and her eastern dominions was therefore based on the 'Singapore Strategy', which would see the British fleet sail from home waters should Singapore be threatened, and arrive within a maximum of 70 days – the time frame known as 'the period before relief'.

General Officer Commanding, Major General Sir William Dobbie, aggressively challenged this theory. He conducted exercises to prove that troops could be landed on Malaya's north-east coast during the monsoon season of 1936-37 and proved that the strategy was not fit for purpose. Furthermore, the monsoon season would not hinder an invasion, but rather act in the invaders' favour, due to cloud cover making air reconnaissance impossible. Dobbie drafted an official communiqué highlighting his concerns, stating that 'It is an attack from the northward that I regard as the greatest potential danger to the fortress. The jungle is not in most places impassable by infantry.'

Dobbie had first perceived the Japanese to be a threat in 1936, when he took command in Malaya. Japan at that time was using every means possible to gather intelligence to prepare for an invasion. There were over 3,000 Japanese in Malay, whose effectiveness and activities were greater than the sum of their parts. Together with Japanese business – notably Nissan and the Japanese Chamber of Commerce – they had a truly integrated intelligence-gathering organisation. In addition, Japanese fishermen undertook marine mapping of coastline and tributaries. The infamous 'Mamasans' – the Madams in Japanese-run brothels – were also tasked to pass on overheard gossip from clients.

The Japanese had also infiltrated the media as journalists, while the official photographer of the Singapore Naval base was later discovered to be a colonel in Japanese intelligence. Malaya and its southern tip, Singapore, back then and as it is now, was a multicultural society, which made such infiltration easier. The Japanese capitalised on exporting every useful detail back home to their high command.

Malaya and Singapore constituted a vital strategic outpost to Great Britain in its prosecution of the war. The mineral wealth in the production of palm oil, tin, and rubber were vital to the war effort. Dobbie knew that if this fell into the enemy's hands, the situation in the east would be changed.

He was also secretly infuriated by the arrogance of the Japanese and their contempt for the British. A man of action, he needed someone of a like mind, who had the skills to infiltrate and neutralise Japanese intelligence gathering and help plan for what might be the worst-case scenario. He sought and found such a person in Hayley Bell, known as an 'old China hand' – due to his intimate knowledge of South-east Asian culture and dynamics – who had been appointed MI5's Security Chief in Singapore. Bell subsequently recruited a small team from the British Army, which included a young officer in the Gordon Highlanders – Captain Ivan Lyon.

His regiment had recently returned from the Japanese mainland, and Lyon was fearful of having to return to a form of regimental servitude. He was not an orthodox soldier, although he came from a family with a strong traditional military background and a very proud lineage. His father had been at the Siege of Ladysmith during the Boer War and had fought with extreme gallantry on the Somme in the Great War, before ending his career as an attaché in the Balkans and Brussels. His son Ivan had been educated at Harrow, Winston Churchill's alma mater. The Lyons' were one of Scotland's most illustrious families, whose lineage could be traced back to the Strathmores and then to King George VI's Consort, Elizabeth Bowes-Lyon. Ivan Lyon's first choice for a military career was the Royal Navy, but he failed his entry examination at Dartmouth. Always irrepressible, he went on to enter Sandhurst, and subsequently joined the Gordon Highlanders.

Lyon was also a gifted sailor. After arriving in Singapore, he and fellow Gordon Highland officer, Francis Moir-Byres, took out a loan and purchased a three-and-a-half ton, single-masted yacht called *Vinette*. Lyon and Moir-Byres, sailing on *Vinette*, became intimate with the islands surrounding Singapore and the east coast of Malaya. Lyon also became a self-taught navigator, who could accurately sail by the stars.

Always seeking new stimulation, one evening Lyon enjoyed an outing with colleagues in downtown Singapore, sampling indigenous delicacies accompanied by an ample quantity of the local ice-cold Tiger beer. He visited a tattoo artist in the city's Little India, emerging after a couple of agonising hours with a tiger's head, in lurid yellow, red, and blue, stretching from his waistband to his upper chest. While alcohol may have played a part, this unorthodox and somewhat defiant act singled Lyon out from the run-of-the-mill officer.

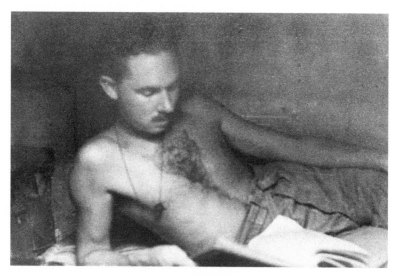

Ivan Lyon with tiger tattoo

The tattoo was to become a source of controversy and conversation amongst officers of the regiment, and when Ivan was asked by a fellow officer to prove or disprove a rumour that he had been tattooed, by displaying his latest alleged acquisition at a mess dinner, he did so with great pride – much to the amusement of the officers in the mess.

Hayley Bell had made an excellent choice in Lyon. A mercurial figure, with a thin moustache, slight build and deeply tanned skin, from a distance he could pass as Asian. He also had the ability to see every problem as a challenge to be solved. His work in the STS was to infiltrate spy networks in Singapore and also train stay-behind teams in sabotage and wireless operations.

Lyon was particularly adept at working undercover. His team quickly penetrated a Japanese spy ring, and substantiated claims that the Japanese were planning to invade both Thailand and Malaya, with plans to move rapidly south. Hayley Bell communicated this intelligence to the high command in Singapore, but it was refuted by the Governor of Singapore, Sir Shenton Thomas, who stated that such propaganda was severely harmful to morale. Sir Thomas maintained the view, consistently shared by others, including the British Minister in Bangkok at that time, Sir Josiah Crosby, that the jungle and the monsoon would make any attempt to take Singapore via Malaya impossible.

Ever irrepressible and tenacious, Hayley Bell ordered Lyon to amass a small force, to demonstrate just how vulnerable Singapore was to the Japanese threat by simulating an attack on the recently completed naval base, under the cover of darkness. The team carried out its task, undetected. Had the attack been real, it would have disabled both the graving dock and floating dock; created a fire that would have destroyed the RAF's fuel dump, sinking a fleet of flying boats moored near RAF HQ; destroyed the switchboard at the civil telephone exchange; and bombed the main power station. The operation, which was a complete success, caused outrage at Government House and Fort Canning, the military HQ in Singapore. Following complaints to the War Office in London, Bell was sacked in May 1939 for his 'unorthodox methods', as 'his small force of intelligence gatherers were using methods not included in any Sandhurst manual to uncover spies and agent provocateurs and, when necessary, imposed summary justice.' Had Bell's warnings to the British Government been heeded and had he been allowed to continue his job as Singapore's Defence Security Officer, the outcome for Singapore may have been very different.

This episode was a disaster for both Hayley Bell and Singapore, but it was to serve Ivan Lyon well. It had left an indelible mark in his mind on the effectiveness of undercover operations. The way in which Hayley Bell had carried out the exercise to highlight Singapore's vulnerability to attack would be a tactic Lyon would not forget, and would use in the future to great effect.

Chapter Two

Beginning of the End

Ever the ladies' man and adventurer, Lyon took time out from his duties to sail single-handedly from Singapore and up the east coast of Malaya, with the intention of reaching an island south of Saigon, the capital of French Indochina. The island was a penal colony where Lyon had been told a young French beauty lived, with her family. This small piece of interesting intelligence had emerged during drinks in the mess with his Regimental Commanding Officer, Willy Graham.

The island was under the control of the Vichy French, who, like their counterparts in France, were collaborators with both the Nazis and the Japanese. It is not known if this voyage was an official operation to allow Lyon to detect and familiarise himself with potential landing sites on the east coast of Malaya and Indochina. However, it is known that at a later date he was tasked to identify such locations, and spent considerable time mapping and making forays ashore to engage with locals and seek intelligence. As a consequence of his adventures, Lyon was to become fluent in Malay and familiar with its culture, enabling him to befriend and develop confidence with local villagers.

While on his solo voyage, Lyon encountered a severe storm to the south of Indochina, sustaining considerable damage to *Vinette*'s sails. However, he was able to find safe harbour on Poulo Condore, the French penal colony, where he was greeted by the Governor, Commandant Georges Bouvier. As Lyon spoke fluent French, the encounter became very convivial, and he was introduced to the Governor's daughter, the young and very beautiful Gabrielle. At that time in her early twenties, she had been married at the age of 16 and was now divorced with a young daughter.

Lyon was immediately captivated by her good looks, cultured manners, and sophistication for one so young. Clearly, Gabrielle also took a considerable liking to Lyon, although she had reservations regarding his capacity to enjoy alcohol in a social setting. While Lyon effected the repairs to his vessel with local support, he did so at a very leisurely pace.

During his stay, it became clear to Lyon that Gabrielle's father was not a puppet of the Vichy French and could be an excellent source of future intelligence. Evidently, the visit was very enjoyable for all concerned, and Lyon managed to spin it out for five days before setting sail to return to Singapore. His encounter would be very beneficial in intelligence terms, and would change his life, as he had fallen deeply in love with Gabrielle. This encounter would be one of the many strands that shaped and determined Lyon's future pathway.

Lyon and Gabrielle were married in Saigon on 7 July 1939, followed by a second regimental ceremony in Singapore. They were quickly established in married quarters in Orchard Road, before moving to a bungalow near Changi. Gabrielle's arrival was something of a sensation for the expat community as, in addition to her youth and natural beauty, she exuded sophistication and culture. While Gabrielle settled into their new home, Ivan continued his work, flitting between his regiment and the intelligence work that he favoured.

When the intelligence network was disbanded in mid-1939, due to Bell's dismissal, Lyon reluctantly accepted a role in the Intelligence Bureau's censorship office. However, it did not last long. Since the fall of France in 1940, Indochina had been in the adminstrative control of the pro-German Vichy French. Lyon's superiors, aware that he spoke fluent French, appointed him *aide-de-camp* to General Catroux, the ousted Governor General of Indochina, a move that could not have been unintentional.

As an SOE operative, Lyon's new appointment would have given him, and SOE, a unique insight into Indochina, its territory and, most importantly, contact with the undercover Free French operatives, who had infiltrated the Vichy French. Gabrielle was also able to support her husband's war effort, working in a senior position for the head of the Free French in Singapore, who closely supported the work of SOE.

Lyon's secret SOE work continued and, in July 1941, Japan invaded Indochina, which immediately resulted in the USA, Britain, and Holland imposing severe economic sanctions that would really bite home, as Japan was totally reliant on exports to run its domestic infrastructure, never mind a growing war machine. The Japanese High Command was now faced with a stark choice, prosecute full-scale war in Asia and capture the necessary resources, or die a slow death.

Back on Poulo Condore, Gabrielle's father Georges had become a vital source of new intelligence regarding Japanese movements, which was passed through Lyon to SOE. Georges Bouvier continued to do this work for some considerable time, with a brave disregard for both his and his wife's safety. Eventually though, the Vichy French detected the flow of information, which led back to the Bouviers. Georges was imprisoned and subsequently subjected to a ferocious beating by the Vichy French, no doubt administered to demonstrate to their Japanese masters their strength of resolve in dealing with what they saw as traitors. Both Georges and his wife, who met the same fate, died of appalling injuries in hospital. Gabrielle's gallant father was later to be awarded the posthumous Cross of Liberation by Charles de Gaulle, leader of the Free French.

Shortly after the Japanese invasion of Indochina, Gabrielle gave birth to a son, Clive. This period must have been a time of very considerable stress for the new parents. Lyon, who was clearly a very committed father and husband, was about to embark on further, more dangerous work for SOE at 101 STS.

On 8 December 1941, without any declaration of war, Japan did what Lyon and others had dreaded, and predicted, for so long.

At 1230 hours they invaded southern Thailand and shelled the beaches of Kota Bahru, on Malaya's far eastern coast, prior to an invasion that would see them establish an iron grip on Malaya. Seventy-eight minutes later, they attacked the United States Fleet at Pearl Harbour where, because of the International Date line, it was still 7 December, catapulting the USA, Britain, Australia, New Zealand and other British Dominions in the South-west Pacific into war with Japan.

At around 0300 hours, the first bombs were dropped on Singapore. The city, ablaze with lights, was an easy target. Sixty-one people were killed, with another 131 seriously injured. The popular department store, Robinson's, in the city centre, was damaged as well as several other buildings, but once the crowds had finished sightseeing, and the wreckage cleared away, life went on as normal. No one seemed to know, or particularly care, that the Japanese were capturing town after town in Malaya and that the British forces were on the run. Even if they reached Singapore, all would be well - after all, the island was an impregnable fortress, protected by its massive guns and by the waterway separating it from Malaya, described by Winston Churchill as 'a splendid moat'.

As the Japanese bulldozered their way down the Malay peninsula in what was to become known as 'Bicycle Blitzkrieg', Lyon realised that the situation in the far east was becoming more dangerous day by day. Fearful for the safety of his wife and child, and with Allied resistance against the Japanese advance collapsing like ninepins, Lyon decided it was high time Gabrielle and Clive left. In mid-January 1942 he obtained passages for them on an evacuation vessel, SS *Narkunda,* an old P & O cruise ship, commissioned in WW1, to take them to Perth, Western Australia.

Following his family's departure, Lyon was able to fully concentrate on his SOE duties. On 31 January, while he was preparing to go up country on a secret reconnaissance mission, he was invited to attend a Gordon Highlanders' Regimental Mess dinner. Following this event, he was ordered to attend an urgent meeting with SOE's Lieutenant Colonel Alan Warren, a summons that brought Lyon some sense of relief, as he was fearful of any move to extract him from his SOE work and send him back to the regimental life and duties that he so disliked.

Warren had a very interesting background. As a qualified naval aviator, he knew the area of South-east Asia intimately from his service in the 1920s, when he flew a bi-plane over the South China Sea as a pirate hunter. Prior to his move to Singapore, he was on a top-secret mission to set up rescue routes for stragglers left behind in France after the evacuation of Dunkirk. On successful completion of his duties there, he proceeded to a rendezvous point to await a safe passage back to England, but the Royal Navy did not turn up. Never a man to be fazed by a situation such as this, Warren purchased a rowing boat from a sympathetic Frenchman and rowed back to England.

His office in Singapore was in the Oriental Mission's eleven-storeyed, art-deco style Cathay Building, Singapore's first, and only, skyscraper. It was from here that, in support of 101 STS at Tanjung Bali, Warren and other SOE personnel trained locals and actioned operatives to commit subterfuge, sabotage and black propaganda. Warren personally led a select group of other undercover operatives, including Lyon, whose main aim was to eliminate enemy agents. These ruthless individuals, given total freedom in their choice of weapons, dress, and *modus operandi*, successfully infiltrated and assassinated a large number of Japanese agents and traitors. Such was Warren's regard for Lyon that he went on record as saying, 'They could keep everyone else as long as I had Lyon working for me.'

At a meeting in the Cathay building on 31 January, Warren opened the conversation with 'Things are going badly, Ivan. You know the islands around the south of Singapore. We must try and keep the lines open through Sumatra, even if we are overrun here. If the worst comes to the worst, we may get part of the army out, and whatever happens we shall want to get people in again. It means food dumps, buttering up natives, and setting up local resistance groups, if we can. I am sending out John Davis, Richard Broome, and Jock Campbell, and I want you to go with them.'

Lyon immediately realised the urgency, given the proximity of the Japanese and imminent threat to Singapore. He also firmly grasped and understood that his experience and conditioning over recent years would mean he had a more than reasonable chance of success in carrying out Warren's plan to establish a supply and escape route through Sumatra.

Lyon now needed to surround himself with like-minded individuals with the range of skills needed to bring off this highly challenging mission. One such man was SOE's Herbert 'Jock' Campbell, a successful rubber plantation manager, who lived in Selangor State on mainland Malaya, where he was a Director of the Socfin Rubber Company. A resident since 1924, Campbell had an intimate knowledge of Malaya, and was fluent in Malay and Tamil – the language used by the Ceylonese, who accounted for most of the plantation estate workers. He had originally served in the King's Own Scottish Borderers and, while not a typical man of action, was an excellent strategic planner.

With his attention for detail, he would be extremely useful to Lyon in establishing the escape route. Campbell, along with another hand-picked SOE member, engineer Lance Corporal Baker, were to take care of the Sumatran end of the proposed route, including the extraction up the Indragiri River. The next stage would be overland, across difficult mountainous terrain to Padang, on Sumatra's west coast.

While Lyon accepted the challenge presented by Warren, he voiced considerable concerns about being evacuated himself. In the preceding days, he had seen first-hand the malaise of servicemen on the edge of desertion, and faint-hearted businessmen skulking around the docks, seeking the first opportunity to escape. He did not want himself or his small team to look as if they were going the same way. He made his argument, but Warren was very insistent. Lyon responded by saying, 'Very well, sir, but if I go out that way now, I'll make damn sure to be one of the first back.'

On 1 February, the day after his meeting with Warren and two weeks before the capitulation of Singapore, Lyon arranged to meet Ron Morris, an SOE operative he had met some time before at

101 STS. Lyon was an astute judge of character and knew the type of self-reliant people he needed in order to maximise his chances of success. Morris was a resolute young Welshman, whose parent regiment was the Royal Army Medical Corps. Seconded to SOE's 101 STS, he confided to Lyon that he was bored and envious of the trainees they were sending up country. Lyon could see that Morris was a quick, sturdy, cheerful, and loyal soldier, with a steady look in his intelligent eyes, who spoke with a reassuringly firm voice in his Rhondda Valley lilt. When Lyon asked if the Welshman wished to join him in his endeavour, Morris leapt at the chance. Little did he know that this work would lead to a long-term relationship with Lyon and expose him to ever-increasing danger.

Ronald Morris RAMC

In late January and early February, the Japanese commenced carpet-bombing of the island. Night bombing was common, but Singapore was still lit up like a candle, as there was no effective blackout. The aircraft, mainly Mitsubishi GM3 bombers, came in multiple V formations. The GM3 was known to have little or no defensive guns to guard it from fighter attack. If Allied fighter strength had been available, the Japanese could have been shot out of the sky. As it was, by early February, Singapore had experienced 80 major raids in 24 days. Firefighting and demolition crews were stretched to the limit. The stench of death hung in the air. Almost as an act of desperation Sir Shenton Thomas, who had previously voiced great concern over arming potential Communists, agreed to allow the Chinese Volunteers, many of whom had come from China to fight the Japanese, to take up arms and join the struggle.

SOE operations were rapidly being disbanded, and all documentation and evidence destroyed at Tanjung Bali and the Cathay Building. If anything were found, it would result in retribution and executions of operatives and also of civilians, with whom they had worked and trained. With 101 disbanded, Morris was hurriedly housed in the Union Jack Club in the city, while the team made last minute plans for the southern extraction, stocking an old Chinese steamer, *Hong Chuan*, moored at Clifford Pier, with provisions and medical supplies.

On 3 February, Morris made his way from the Union Jack Club, passing Raffles Hotel, where the doormen, dressed in their distinctive livery, were still welcoming guests. The whole situation seemed surreal, Singapore was being bombed flat, the Japanese were knocking at the door, and yet people were still clinging to the hope that a miracle would deliver them to safety. As Morris proceeded further towards the port and docks, the situation became markedly worse. The destruction there, inflicted by repeated Japanese bombing, was immense. Bodies, and body parts, were scattered everywhere. Local Chinese and Malays were sobbing and in despair. Their homes, businesses, and livelihoods had been destroyed. While the British had not been the greatest of Colonial rulers, the local population knew in their hearts that much worse lay in wait.

Nearing Clifford Pier, Morris could see *Hong Chuan,* a white mist trailing from its heavily soiled funnel, a sure sign that they were preparing to get underway. Crossing the gangplank, he was greeted by Lyon and Campbell, who welcomed him aboard.

Lyon then asked, 'You ready for a bit of an adventure, Taffy?'

Hong Chuan was crewed by four local Chinese and Malays, who hurriedly cast off before turning their attention to the temperamental boiler. As they moved away from the pier and headed out to the main Channel, there was an immediate lifting of tension among both the ship's crew and the SOE contingent. Clearing Pulau Blakang Mati and its 15-inch gun emplacements, they then turned south, heading for Pulau Tjombol.

Ivan Lyon stood at the stern. Behind him, the whole city seemed aglow from the constant bombings and resulting fires. As they proceeded at a moderate pace, he looked back at Keppel Harbour where, in a number of days, the evacuation would start in earnest. He thought of his regimental colleagues, who were preparing to make a stand against the Japanese and felt a degree of guilt for not standing side by side with them. Ironically, more Gordon Highlanders would die in despicable conditions as POWs than in battle.

However, the task at hand for Lyon and his small and capable team was to try to ensure escapees would have the best chance of survival. Lyon knew these waters and the many islands that dotted them exceptionally well. He couldn't help thinking that, if the worst did come to the worst, this knowledge might help them to strike back.

Further south, they cruised along the coast of Sugibawah Island and onto Pulau Durian, off the coast of Sumatra, the island hub where evacuees and casualties could be collected and arrangements made for their onward transit.

The planned route for evacuees, once they reached Durian, was south along the Sumatran coast and then up the vast Indragiri River, which stretches more than 480 kilometres inland to Rengat, the last point to which boats could navigate. From here, the route was to continue overland some 250 kilometres to the port of Padang, where the Royal Navy would transport those lucky enough to have survived to Ceylon or mainland India.

The team visited islands and their small kampongs (villages), and engaged the elders. Lyon was the most fluent in Malay and used his natural charm to explain that they may be able to assist in helping evacuees by taking them to Pulau Durian, where rations and further details would be issued to help them escape further south and, hopefully, to Sumatra. Campbell ensured the goodwill of the locals with seemingly never-ending amounts of cash.

After completing the initial work in setting up food dumps and identifying locals who would assist along the route, Lyon, Morris, Campbell and Baker returned to Singapore on 5 February. Approaching the island, they could see a large ocean liner ablaze near the entrance to Keppel Harbour. They would later learn that it was *Empress of Asia,* which was carrying troops, arms, and munitions. Attacked by nine Japanese dive-bombers, the ship, which was severely damaged, had caught fire and sunk. Unfortunately, some of the weapons on board were to arm 2,000 Chinese men, known as Dalforce, who had been recruited and trained to fight with the Allied soldiers. Two companies would be positioned alongside advanced elements of 8 Australian Division. With their weapons at the bottom of the sea, the Chinese warriors were pitched into battle with obsolete breech-loading rifles, with only five rounds of ammunition each. Tragically, every one of them involved in fighting off the initial assault by the Japanese would be killed in the battle.

Ever since they left Singapore, Lyon had been very concerned over the safety of his wife Gabrielle and baby Clive. Crossing the Indian Ocean, where German raiders, disguised as vessels from a friendly nation, was fraught with danger. Consequently, on his return to the Cathay Building, it was with great relief that he learned of their safe arrival in Fremantle, Perth's port.

Hong Chuan was commandeered for other SOE work, so the next day, 6 February, Lyon, Campbell, Morris, and Baker set about trying to find a way of getting back onto the escape route. During their trip to the Indragiri, Morris had realised that a plentiful quantity of medical supplies was essential, as evacuees would present with a range of injuries needing treatment, requiring a supply of dressings, bandages and splints, as well as the means to cleanse contaminated wounds. He went off in search of supplies and was successful, through previous contacts, in securing considerable amounts of the items he needed. A truck was commandeered and the contents delivered to the dock, where his colleagues had managed to secure a passage on SS *Krain*, being used to evacuate SOE personnel to Rangoon, in Burma. It took most of the afternoon to load the vessel.

The atmosphere was frenetic, with shells constantly landing and exploding all around them but, thankfully, not on them. With the cargo of food and supplies being finally stored ready for embarkation, Morris detected where the medical supplies had been stowed and familiarised himself thoroughly with the inventory. He had a grim feeling that the supplies were going to be put to good use and wanted to be sure that he could lay his hands on the right kit in a timely fashion.

With *Krain*'s loading completed, the vessel steamed up and got underway. Morris noted that the situation had significantly deteriorated in the harbour, with ships and boats under constant attack from Japanese bombers and fighters. It was not long before *Krain* was identified by Japanese aircraft and sustained some damage, resulting in minor casualties, all of which Morris was able to adequately deal with. All of this was taking its toll on the crew and, to further add to the tension, thuds could be heard against the hull of the vessel. Looking over the side, Morris saw bloated dead bodies were striking the bow and being swept along the side, and then astern.

In spite of the damage, *Krain* continued on its way to drop Lyon and Morris off at Pulau Durian, which was now feeling like a safe haven to both. Campbell and Baker remained on the vessel, disembarking at Prigi Radja. *Krain* then picked up further SOE personnel in Sumatra, before setting sail for Rangoon.

Chapter Three

The Sumatran Escape Route

Back on Pulau Durian, Lyon and Morris busied themselves taking the large quantity of stores left on the shore up a jungle track to the top of a hill. The weather in February in Indonesia was almost a constant monsoon, which made the lugging of supplies and the setting up of logistic dumps an arduous pursuit.

With the task complete, and leaving Morris to mind the shop, Lyon set about visiting surrounding islands and kampongs, informing headmen that evacuees should be directed to Durian. Now that the preparations were complete, the pair had plenty of spare time to relax, and think. Morris sat on top of the hill at night, looking in amazement at the phosphorescent sea. Deep in contemplation, his thoughts drifted back to his native Wales where, what now seemed such a short time ago, he had been a coal miner, just like generations of Morrises before him.

He had worked one mile below ground. As a young 14-year-old, he had travelled down into the bowels of the earth, a flat cap on his head and carrying a miner's lamp, a pick and sack to gather coal from a 45-centimetre seam. In the depths of winter, Morris went down the mine in the dark and came up at nightfall, never seeing the light of day. Once, he had been trapped underground when a cave in blocked his exit to the main shaft. Keeping his head, he had crawled for more than 1.5 kilometres to a neighbouring pit, from where he made his escape. There were often accidents underground, some of them serious, and this led him to become a qualified St John's Ambulance first aider.

After working as a miner for five years Morris, aged 19, had applied to join the regular Army in 1938, prior to the declaration of war. On enlistment, his medical skills were identified and he was posted to the Royal Army Medical Corps. The regimental motto was *In Arduis Fidelis*, 'Faithful in Adversity'. Morris lived up to these words in every way and the tough self-reliance he had learned in the mines saw him recruited to SOE.

While Morris perhaps took his character traits for granted, Lyon did not, aware that it was toughness, forged through conditioning, that helped men like Morris do extraordinary things and react calmly under pressure. For his part, the Welshman felt at ease with Lyon, recognising his qualities as a true leader. Morris, who smoked cigarettes, was amazed at how Lyon could go into an almost meditative state, sucking on his trusted pipe. He could almost hear tumblers in Lyon's mind dropping into place as he sat beside him on top of the hill, viewing the mayhem as bombers attacked ships and vessels fleeing from Singapore. Sometime later, Lyon would confide to Morris what his future plans were but, for now, they must focus on assisting those in need, and to try to ensure that, when the time came, those involved in helping others could also escape and not fall into the hands of the Japanese.

On the top of their hill, Lyon and Morris had sensibly constructed an atap hut from palm leaves to shelter them from both the sun and torrential monsoonal rain, which the erratic tropical weather delivered in equal measure. They felt that Warren's choice of nominating Durian as a hub would work well, and this would prove to be so, with many people passed on to the pair, and then onwards to Sumatra. However, as no refugees had yet arrived, in the evening they sat on the hill, looking towards Singapore as they shared a bottle of 'for medicinal purposes' whisky. Throughout the night, as they kept watch, in turn, for both survivors and Japanese in the Durian Straits, they could hear the sound of constant artillery and bombing coming from the direction of Singapore.

One evening, Morris was keeping watch while Lyon earned some well-deserved sleep, only to be abruptly awoken by Morris, who thought the game was up. Clutching his trusted Sten gun, he explained that he had heard what sounded like bodies crashing through the jungle. Instructing Morris to cover him, Lyon crawled forward and disappeared into the dense undergrowth. On hearing strange noises, he sent a rock flying in that direction and, to his relief, heard the intruders scampering away. Following their path with his torch, he saw to his surprise that they were wild pigs. The incident created a degree of laughter and merriment, but neither Morris nor Lyon would openly admit that things were becoming tense, with notably increased enemy activity around the islands. Little did they know things were about to become a lot worse.

On Friday, 13 February, Morris and Lyon looked on in amazement as HMS *Durban*, SS *Empire Star*, HMS *Kedah*, an anti-submarine ship, and MV *Gordon,* a cargo ship, crammed with evacuees and all moving at maximum speed, passed Durian. During their passage through the straits, the ships manoeuvred violently, as they came under constant attack by Japanese bombers. Over a period of four hours, the convoy was attacked by a total of 64 bombers. However, although all apart from *Gorgon* were damaged, and a number of passengers and crew were killed, the vessels managed to make the port of Tanjung Priok – near Batavia, the capital of Java. Literally thousands of people who reached safety that day owed their lives to the brave actions of their ships' crews.

That same day, Friday 13 February, which would become known as 'Black Friday', HMS *Kuala*, *Tien Kwang,* and *Kung Wo* – Chinese riverboats and steamers – were ordered to assist with the Singapore evacuation. *Kuala,* commanded by Captain Caithness, embarked 500 civilians, of which 250 were women and children. The following morning, *Kuala*, along with various other ships packed with refugees, sought shelter close to the island of Pompong. However, Japanese aircraft heading for Java soon spotted the ships and approximately 40 planes detached from the main formation to attack the virtually defenceless vessels. *Kuala* suffered a direct hit on the bridge and caught fire. Planes bombed and strafed the stricken craft all morning, even firing at refugees struggling in the water. Those who made landfall also didn't escape their attention.

A total of 700 survivors reached Pompong Island, where they huddled in the jungle with no food, awaiting rescue. The first to be picked up were 130 women and children, the following day, but their joy was short-lived. The vessel, little more than a barge, was bombed and only three people survived. Others who reached the island died from their injuries. However, other vessels that came to the rescue of the remainder of the castaways there and on various islands, ferried the survivors to Jock Campbell in Sumatra.

Morris and Lyon realised that, as the situation in Singapore deteriorated and more tried to flee, things were about to become a great deal worse. They did not have long to wait for the expected mass exodus to move southwards, but the Japanese anticipated this and stepped up the attacks. Smaller and much slower vessels that fled Singapore on Black Friday came under constant attack and bombardment. Unable to outrun the bombs, many were sunk or disabled.

Survivors from the bombing arrived on Durian, where they were assisted by Lyon and Morris. Morris's medical skills kept him busy, as many of those who came ashore had severe injuries, suffering from cuts, contusions and fractures. He set about making splints, setting broken bones, stemming bleeding, suturing gashes and removing shrapnel and chunks of wood embedded in their flesh. All without anaesthetic. All he had to offer was his comforting voice, softly whispering and sometimes humming *Men of Harlech,* which appeared to bring some calm. There were many deeply distressed and orphaned children, to whom Morris and Lyon tried to bring some reassurance. At the end of the day, once they had done the best they could with the living, they turned to digging graves to give those beyond help a dignified burial. Somehow, Morris then managed to find the energy to raid the rations and in no time at all had a cauldron of stew bubbling.

The work undertaken by the SOE team saved hundreds stranded on the islands during this period and, on Durian, Lyon and Morris worked tirelessly for days on end without a break. They had no time to think of their own welfare, there were too many desperate and injured people who needed comfort and help. Time and again, they had the sad task of burying the dead, in an ever-expanding clearing in the undergrowth. The death toll that weighed so heavily on them would later strengthen their resolve to avenge the wanton barbarity of the Japanese.

On Tuesday 17 February two ships and a motor launch arrived at Durian with bad news. Singapore had surrendered.

As the tumultuous days of February 1942 drew to a close, survivors arriving on Durian became fewer, and the Japanese presence on the surrounding islands more prolific. Lyon made arrangements with locals to transfer any further survivors across to the Indragiri River, where they would be ferried upstream on the now well-established rescue route. As the pair clambered down the steep track from the top of the island and their little hut, which had served them so well, little did Morris know that Lyon had plans to return.

They climbed carefully aboard their small sailing vessel, maintaining as much silence as possible in the darkness, and headed off towards the south. All was well until some hours later when, in the early hours of the morning, they heard the pounding of a ship's engine, then saw the silhouette of a destroyer some distance away. It appeared to be closing and, as they were fairly certain that by now friendly vessels had disappeared, they feared the worst. With the destroyer on their port bow, they rapidly steered to starboard whilst reefing down the sail. Grabbing the oars they then gently paddled away, undetected, in the other direction.

They were breathing a sigh of relief when, to their horror, another destroyer appeared on the starboard bow and swept a searchlight across the surface of the water. With the tide running with them, the pair crouched low in the boat and said several silent prayers. They were certain they had been spotted and that the destroyer was coming to take a closer look but, incredibly, the lookouts did not see the boat, drifting on the current. It was with great relief that they were able to hoist the sail and continue on their way.

The waves now started to slap against the hull, and the sail started to bite, indicating freshening weather and wind in their favour. However, the benevolent wind turned into a violent storm, which sent the sea churning and propelled the small boat, driven before the wind, on a roller coaster ride. Lyon, at the tiller, was in his element. When Morris asked, 'Do you want to get some sleep, and I will take the tiller?, Lyon calmly replied, 'No thanks, we should both get some sleep.'

He then extracted the tiller, placed it on the deck, curled up and, to Morris's amazement, seemed to immediately drop off to sleep. Such was their fatigue and the stress and strain of the last few weeks, along with the recent encounter with the destroyers, that Morris too fell deeply asleep, rocked by the motion of the sea. Dawn broke and they awoke, amazingly refreshed, to a still restless sea and no land in sight. As the sun broke through the cloud cover, directly above them, indicating midday, they spotted the mouth of the Indragiri. Entering the river, they made for Tembilahan, before sailing on to meet Campbell at Rengat. Whilst docking there, they uncharacteristically nudged a boat moored alongside the small wharf. Morris and Lyon almost dived for cover as a rich Australian voice berated them from the wheelhouse with every expletive known to mankind, questioning their seamanship and parentage.

They had bumped into *Kofuku Maru*, captained by straight-talking Bill Reynolds, who had been busily rescuing evacuees on a small Japanese fishing boat he had found abandoned in Singapore. Sailing towards the Riau islands in Indonesia, he had avoided 'bomb alley' and the Durian Strait, to deliver hundreds of Dutch refugees from the Indonesian island of Bintan into the safe hands of the Dutch Controller at Rengat. There, Reynolds had heard about the hundreds of people shipwrecked near Pompong and was now acting as a lifeline, shuttling them to safety. He had done this with ease as *Kofuku Maru*, barely 21 metres in length, had been built in Japan in the 1930s and in these waters blended in perfectly.

Despite Reynolds' outburst, Lyon was drawn instinctively to the rugged, weather-beaten Australian. Born in Victoria, in south-eastern Australia in 1892, he had served with the Royal Navy in the Great

War on the Dover Patrol. After obtaining his Master's Ticket in Scotland in 1918, he had been a merchant mariner for years and had vast experience sailing in Asian waters. Although Morris, caught unawares by the verbal onslaught issuing from Reynolds' mouth, was slightly apprehensive as the tall, lanky figure approached, Lyon was completely unfazed. In fact, Lyon was fascinated by Reynolds, a man larger than life.

In reply to the Australian's outburst Lyon asked 'Hello, and how are you?' a response that saw them all break into laughter. Reynolds then invited them on board *Kofuku Maru*. After spending the last 24 hours on the ocean in an open sailboat, the little fishing boat felt like luxury. Reynolds extracted a hidden bottle of whisky, which they enjoyed while they discussed their next move, Reynolds to pick up more castaways and Morris and Lyon to take the long route across the mountains from Rangat to Padang, where they hoped to make their escape in advance of the Japanese army now making its way south to Sumatra.

They learned of Bill's many exploits, and the hundreds of people he had already rescued and given safe passage. As the Japanese had not taken any notice of him so far, Reynolds announced that, once his rescue work was completed, he was going to sail *Kofuku Maru* through the heavily defended waters of the Malacca Straits, then across the Indian Ocean to India. There was no one to stop him. He was a free agent. He had stockpiled food and fuel for his escape from Singapore and rescue missions, all of which were undertaken without any orders and of his own volition.

Reynolds also voiced his incredulity that, in his journeys to and fro to the islands, his tatty little fishing boat had attracted no attention from the Japanese. This was the catalyst for an idea already forming in Lyon's mind. For it to work he needed both Reynolds and his fishing boat. It was a seemingly audacious, crazy idea, but when he ran it past Reynolds in total secrecy, the adventurous Australian embraced it with enthusiasm.

Leaving Reynolds to finish his rescue work and begin his perilous journey to India, Morris, Campbell, and Lyon, riding in an open car that Campbell had acquired, made their way across the mountains over quite terrifying roads, with sheer drops into what seemed to be oblivion. As they progressed higher into the mountains, the rain and mist became icy cold. The journey took longer than expected, as Campbell and Lyon engaged with Dutch Army officers and civil servants, who were there as part of the Dutch East Indies protectorate, the objective being to ensure that the escape route stayed open for as long as possible.

Coming down out of the mountains and into the coastal settlement of Padang, and its normally sleepy port of Emmahaven, they were faced with masses of desperate evacuees scavenging for food wherever they could find it, sleeping rough, and awaiting transport to take them to freedom across the Indian Ocean. With frequent bombing attacks on the port, there was an air of inevitability and desperation that, with a rapidly advancing Japanese army and total air superiority, they might be captured. As if they had not been through enough already.

Colonel Warren, who was in charge of the evacuations, had arranged for a submarine to take SOE members to India. In anticipation, Morris, Campbell, and Lyon scoured the harbour at Emmahaven and stood on watch, but the submarine never did arrive. However, a small 600-ton Dutch steamer, SS *Palopo,* was rapidly readying itself for departure.

Warren felt this might be the very last ship to leave Padang. His instincts told him that the remaining refugees, waiting desperately on the quayside of the harbour for rescue, would be almost certainly spending the rest of the war as POWs. Realising that Morris's medical skills could be put to good use, Warren facilitated his passage on board, along with other SOE operatives. Although the vessel was already overcrowded, another 50 people also filed on board – 38 servicemen and 12 civilians. Among them were British and Australian soldiers and sailors, Indian Army officers and also Colonel Arthur Cummings, Indian Army, who had been awarded a Victoria Cross for his extraordinary courage during the Malayan Campaign. Although Campbell and Lyon could have joined the 50 on board *Palopo,* Warren ordered them to stay behind. He had some ideas about how these two – Lyon, the competent sailor, and

Campbell with his organisational ability – could help with further possible evacuation.

Little did the passengers departing on *Palopo* know that they were to be the very last to escape from Padang in a motorised vessel. Nor did they realise what a perilous journey lay ahead. However, there was low cloud cover, which pleased *Palopo*'s Master, as it would give them a good chance of evading enemy attack. As the small ship cast off, Morris waved farewell to Campbell and Lyon, his now close companions, wondering when, and if, he would ever see them again.

Morris then reported to the bridge to ask if he could assist in tending to the injured and sick. Delighted that his offer was accepted, he set to work bringing aid and comfort to those who had been through so much suffering. He was also aware that being busy provided a positive distraction from the very real danger that the ship was going to be in, for some considerable time. As *Palopo*'s pistons gave out a reassuringly steady and slow beat, they sailed north-west, weaving their way past the islands off the coast, through the Siberut Straits towards the open ocean.

Moving through the many passengers on board, Morris discovered that they were sharing the voyage with survivors of the doomed *Prince of Wales* and *Repulse,* who by now must have felt they had been to hell and back. Below deck, searching in the subdued light as he made his way among the many injured and sick, he came across a British nurse. Recognising her bloodstained and tattered uniform as that of the Queen Alexandra's Imperial Military Nursing Corps, Morris checked her over. He was mystified, as he could not find any cuts or contusions to account for the condition of her blood stained uniform, but she was extremely fatigued and fragile. He spoke gently in his soft and calming Welsh voice, holding the back of her head to help her take a sip of some warm and comforting tea. She seemed keen to share her experiences with someone who appeared to be gentle and caring. Morris instinctively understood that, for her, even though she was exceptionally frail, this might be a cathartic experience and as good as any medicine he could provide.

Morris sat by her silently as she recounted her story for the first time. He soon had tears rolling down his face and felt a deep and burning anger. On 14 February, the day before Singapore surrendered, she had been working as a ward nurse at the Alexandra Military Hospital, tending the sick and injured, when Japanese troops burst into the ward in what she described as a highly excited and almost frenzied state. When a Japanese soldier with a bayoneted rifle came towards her screaming unintelligibly, a sergeant in the Royal Army Medical Corps, who had been assisting her with her rounds, stepped in front of her and put his hands up to protect her. The soldier thrust his bayonet straight through the sergeant's thorax and, as the man stumbled to the floor, stabbed him in the back. The nurse fell onto the sergeant's prostrate form in a futile attempt to protect him, not realising there was nothing she could do. The Japanese soldiers then went on to commit similar atrocities in the operating theatre, murdering surgeons along with their patients.

The young nurse leaned against the bulkhead, sobbing deeply. Morris placed his arm around her, cradling her head to bring what little comfort he could. He stared into space, his cheeks soaked with tears and burning with a depth of anger that he had never before experienced. On returning to his regiment after the war, Morris was to learn that troops from the Japanese 18th Division, who were responsible for the massacre, had entered the hospital and bayoneted more than 50 patients, nurses, and doctors. Tragically, many of the patients killed were survivors from *Prince of Wales* and *Repulse*. Japanese officers had then ordered the 200 surviving patients and staff to be locked in a small building nearby. Anyone who staggered and fell was bayoneted. Some died overnight. The enemy troops killed the remainder, apart from five who managed to escape, the next day.

The Japanese justification for their actions was that Indian troops guarding the hospital had fired at them from within the hospital grounds, thus breaching the Geneva Convention. Ironically, after the war, when trying to extricate themselves from allegations of other atrocities they had committed, all against the

Geneva Convention, the Japanese stated that Japan did not abide by the Convention, as it had never been ratified by their parliament.

As *Palopo*'s Dutch master weaved his way northwest, the passengers learned that Colombo in Ceylon was to be their destination. However, it soon became clear that the Japanese, realising that the escape route was from Padang across the Indian Ocean, had ordered bombers to attack and sink vessels carrying survivors. *Palopo* had no means of defence, other than the soldiers with their rifles and limited amounts of ammunition. With the ship proceeding at an excruciatingly slow rate of eight knots, Morris looked over the side to see the remains of a ship, parts of which were floating in the water, along with decaying and bloated bodies. The local Malay crewmen thought it might be what was left of a Dutch vessel, their sister ship SS *Rooseboom,* which had left Padang a week prior to their embarkation – a revelation that exacerbated the already frayed nerves of the survivors on board *Palopo*. The assumption that the ship was *Rooseboom* was confirmed the following day when, while sailing through a calm sea in excruciatingly hot and humid weather, they came across a raft containing two survivors. Once on board, the two rescued Javanese sailors confirmed they were from *Rooseboom*. They also stated that they thought they were the only remaining survivors of the hundreds of passengers who had left Padang.

The ship had been attacked by Japanese submarine I-59, commanded by an ambitious young naval officer, Lieutenant Yoshimatsui. The vessel had capsized, and sank rapidly, giving the crew time to launch only one lifeboat. Designed to hold 28 people, it had 80 crammed into it. Another 135 were in the water. Years later, evidence would come to light of unspeakable acts by some of those who survived the sinking. They included British Army deserters and Javanese crew members, who killed fellow survivors, drinking their blood and eating their flesh, before they were eventually forced over the side by other castaways, where they deservedly met their fate. After many weeks drifting at sea, only two of the ill-fated *Rooseboom*'s passengers survived.

On 11 March *Palopo* arrived in Ceylon, where Morris disembarked and reported to his regiment, which posted him to Number 55 Combined Military Hospital in Columbo. He was worried about Campbell and Lyon, as it was now apparent that no further ships had reached Ceylon from Sumatra. After *Palopo* left Padang, the Japanese had closed to within 65 kilometres of the port, effectively holding the high ground and preventing further escapes.

Ever since the Japanese had arrived in the Dutch East Indies, officials and the military had tried to remain neutral, in the hope of clinging onto their far-eastern empire and lifestyle. But they underestimated the Japanese ruthlessness. Initially, most Indonesians joyfully welcomed the Japanese as liberators from their Dutch colonial masters. The sentiment changed, however, as Indonesians realised they were expected to endure hardship for the Japanese war effort.

As the Japanese were due to come down out of the mountains to the east of Padang, as an act of compliance Dutch officials ordered the port to be blocked to stop any further vessels from leaving. With the situation rapidly worsening and no support from the Dutch, Colonel Warren, who had now met up with Lyon and Campbell, secured a perahu, *Sederhana Djohanes* – a type of sailing boat common in Malaya and Indonesia that could be sailed with either end at the front and which, typically, has a large triangular sail and an outrigger. Warren, who had an eye for a vessel that would blend into the local scene, purchased the boat with money from his war chest. He then had it provisioned and moored up the coast to the north.

Warren was receiving reports of a total breakdown in discipline, in and around the port, with reports of rape and officers mutineering further adding to the chaos. As a highly moral officer and a man of great integrity, he decided he must stay to try to maintain discipline and some order.

The party selected to sail on *Sederhana Djohanes* was made up of 16 naval and military personnel, six with a connection to SOE, including Lyon and Campbell. Also in the party were two Malay servants, Jamal and Lo Gnap Soon, brought along by Broom and Davis. Colonel Warren, realising that the timing of their departure was critical to avoid capture or attack, ordered them to sail under cover of darkness on the night of 8 March. After a nerve-wracking journey in small, horse-drawn carts in driving rain, they arrived at the sleepy local fishing village of Perjalanan, where *Sederhana Djohanes* was moored offshore. Several men, including Lyon and three fishermen employed to act as crew, rowed out to inspect their acquisition. Lyon cast a critical eye over the vessel, which he estimated was about 14 metres at the waterline and had a beam of about five metres. At first glance, it had the look of a ketch. There was a triangular shelter made of atap, and two masts of six and nine metres, able to carry a very large head of sail, with a fore, jib, and mizzen. *Sederhana Djohanes* also had the biggest bowsprit Lyon had ever seen on a boat of that size.

On further and more detailed inspection, he established she had no keel, as she was used for coastal and river trading and was not designed for the open ocean. A vessel with no keel could not sail close to the wind, so the only way to keep her stable would be to sail with a prevailing wind, goose-winged. Although Lyon had great reservations about the condition of the sails and ropes and the lines that operated them, he kept these thoughts to himself, not wishing to cause further anxiety in what was already a fraught situation. However, it was a boat and, as he reminded himself, 'beggars can't be choosers'.

Reporting back to the others, waiting on the shore, Lyon gave a highly optimistic report. They agreed that Colonel Warren had done exceptionally well, and felt they had much for which to be grateful. The provisions Warren had loaded on board included tinned meat, fish, biscuits, tea, coffee and rice. Fresh water was stored in drums and a quick calculation revealed that it would be sufficient for half a litre per crew member for 42 days at sea – not a lot in such tropical conditions.

Lyon was also secretly worried about the expected prevailing weather conditions in the coming weeks. The north-east winds and monsoon were about to give way to south-west driven winds, which would also be accompanied by severe monsoonal rain. While studying local sea conditions back in Singapore, Lyon had learned that the great tea clippers of the 19th century never set sail for England at this time of year. This knowledge did not fill him with confidence but, again, he kept these thoughts very much to himself.

The boat's skipper was an elderly fisherman called Bapa (father), who revealed that the vessel had actually never sailed at night and had no lights. Bapa was clearly not comfortable with this situation but nevertheless set sail towards the north-west. During the early part of the passage, the boat was twice attacked by Japanese planes patrolling overhead. When the alarm was raised the Malay crew, plus Jamal and Lo, stayed on deck while the British members crammed, as best they could, into the limited space under the atap shelter and below deck in the hope that the locals would be seen simply as native fishermen.

When Lyon explained to the skipper and crew that their destination was Ceylon, there were some furtive exchanges in their mother tongue. As it became very clear that they were distraught at the thought of continuing on what they felt to be a suicide mission, they were dropped off on an island just off the coast and recompensed for their trouble. Before he said farewell, Bapa conducted some form of religious service, blessing the crew and the frail *Sederhana Djohanes*.

They were going to need all the help they could get. During the night, as they continued to sail a north-westerly course, the boat hit a severe squall and developed a frightening roll, which almost sent their water supply overboard. However, after the sails were reduced the vessel was brought under control. Perversely, in the morning the sea was dead calm and, although the crew tried several sail variations to catch what little wind there was, it became clear that the sails and rigging were in a precarious state and had been damaged. Consideration was given to putting into the island of Nias to undertake repairs, but sterling efforts by several crew members, armed with sewing kits, managed to repair most of the damage.

When Lyon's fears on the boat's handling were confirmed, he designed a unique instrument with a pendulum and two parallel lines. On it was inscribed the message, 'If the pendulum swings past these lines, the vessel will capsize', a sobering message to anyone taking the tiller who was not experienced.

Lyon had brought with him a school atlas and highly valued chronometer, a gift from his Auntie Buzz for his 21st birthday. By March 12 they had sailed almost 180 nautical miles from Padang and turned the vessel to a more westerly direction, making for the open sea and Ceylon, which Lyon calculated to be 1,000 nautical miles away. During the days that followed, they experienced force seven gales, and at one point covered 26 miles in two hours in what one crew member recollected as a 'rollercoaster ride'.

By the end of the first week, they had sailed 300 miles and, on 18 March, Lyon announced in his normal calm and reassuring way the welcome news that they had covered 96 miles in the last 24 hours. But the joy was short-lived when a Japanese reconnaissance aircraft came to take a far closer look. Jamal took the tiller and waved, whilst the rest took cover. Eventually, the aircraft turned and disappeared, the ever-decreasing engine noise a sound of welcome reassurance.

Campbell, who had been put in charge of rations, supplied what at best could be described as three fairly frugal meals per day. The worry was the water supply. In an attempt to help the crew understand the need to preserve it in order to maintain their chances of survival, Campbell doled it out, half a mug at a time. When the boat was becalmed for several days on a flat calm sea with no wind, just the occasional flap of a sail to break the monotony, the crew sweltered and suffered. Morale was sinking rapidly, and it was only Lyon's steadfast and single-minded leadership that gave those on board some degree of confidence to continue.

However, this weather was soon replaced by burgeoning black clouds. As the wind picked up, Lyon ordered the mizzen and jib to be lowered, as his instincts told him they were about to face the possibility of a much more dangerous development – a waterspout, the epicentre of a small but potentially highly damaging cyclone, which was sucking the sea from a radius of 15 metres and into a cone that disappeared above them. The boat yawed and bucked over waves for the next 24 hours, with the crew literally clinging to the deck and ropes to stay on board. When the storm eventually abated and Lyon was able to take some navigational readings, he announced they had actually been pushed back by two miles. This had a further and devastating effect on morale, which was exacerbated when crew members came out in what Jamal called 'busuk', or suppurating sores. By 28 March, a fresh breeze had sprung up, raising everyone's hopes, only to plummet almost immediately when a Japanese bomber approached and opened fire with its machine gun, with several rounds striking the boat. The plane returned on several occasions to deliver repeated bursts but, to everyone's astonishment, no-one was injured. Fortunately, for the next few days an easterly wind drove them in the right direction towards Ceylon.

They were some 250 miles from their destination when an aircraft engine was heard, leading to the belief that it must be the RAF. Everyone waved and shouted, until they saw it was Japanese. This led to further apprehension and uncertainty, was it from a carrier, or had Ceylon fallen to the enemy? Hopes continued to be raised, then dashed, when they saw several tankers that they thought would come to their rescue. Thankfully, the boat's profile was small and they were not sighted by the lookouts, as the ships were Japanese vessels that had captured other British escapees when they were in sight of Ceylon.

The men sailed on with their spirits and morale at an all-time low. They thought they could hear another tropical storm approaching but it was the sound of two major warships engaged in battle, the British aircraft carrier HMS *Hermes,* and its escort, the V-Class Australian destroyer *Vampire.* The vessels had been ordered to Trincomalee, the principal port on the east coast of Ceylon, from where it was planned that they would become part of a task force to attack the Vichy French in Madagascar. However, the Japanese Navy now had control of the entire Bay of Bengal and the vessels had come under attack from a powerful enemy fleet of five carriers, four battleships, two heavy and one light cruiser, and 11 destroyers. Accompanying the fleet were six refueling tankers. These were the vessels that the party on *Sederhana Djohanes* had sighted earlier, in the mistaken belief that they were Allied ships.

The Japanese launched a force of 85 Dive Bombers, escorted by nine Zero fighters, onto the vulnerable *Hermes* and *Vampire*. *Hermes* was first to be sunk, taking an unprecedented 40 direct hits and killing 307 men, including the captain, Richard F J Onslow. *Vampire* met the same fate, with the captain and seven others killed. The Japanese only suffered minor losses, losing four bombers. Prior to this, in preparation for an anticipated attack on Colombo, the Deputy Commander-in-Chief had ordered HM Ships *Dorsetshire* and *Cornwall* to sea. Both were spotted and attacked by Japanese aircraft, going to the bottom within 15 minutes. The losses inflicted by the Japanese on the British Fleet since early December 1942 were now considerable.

Chapter Four

Land at Last

In an attempt to fix their location and ascertain if they were sailing towards capture or freedom, frantic efforts were being made on board *Sederhana Djohanes* to repair their only radio, which had been out of action for many days. Finally, a signal was picked up, allowing them to establish they were still 100 nautical miles east of Ceylon. Even at this late stage of the voyage, which was now into its sixth week, could hardly be called uneventful. When the crew heard a pronounced splash and scream, they discovered that SOE's Brian Passmore had fallen overboard. Spotting the triangular fin of a shark closing in on him, he swam frantically towards the vessel, where a tense crew hauled his exhausted body on to the deck, just in time.

At long last, on 12 April, and after 34 long days at sea, land was sighted – the mountains that lay about 80 kilometres to the east of Colombo. Although no one had any idea if they were sailing into Japanese or British hands, the crew members finally felt they had something to celebrate. However, that night there was a further mishap when Douglas Fraser, a civilian member of the team, jumped up to free the foresheet, slipped and fell overboard, catching his chin on the anchor as he went and sustaining a gaping wound. Gushing with blood, he too had to be hauled on board. While his shipmates held him down, 'Doc' Davies, of the RAMC, sutured the ragged tissues together using sailmakers' twine and a suitably thick needle, certainly not designed for surgical procedures and without the benefit of anaesthesia.

Due to the length of the voyage, under extreme conditions in a cramped vessel hardly designed for such a journey, tempers were bound to become frayed. Lyon, who had emerged as the natural leader, suggested a surprise and victorious entry into Colombo Harbour, an option favoured by the sailors, but not the army personnel, given the uncertainty over the occupancy of the port. Following heated exchanges, it was decided to attempt a covert landing instead. Tensions rose again as Lyon sailed towards the shoreline in a bid to beach the vessel, the non-swimmers favoured a proper mooring or jetty. However, he quickly turned the boat through 180 degrees when cries of alarm warned of impending danger, in the form of extremely jagged rocks protruding from the breaking water.

As Lyon headed in the opposite direction in order to find a safe landing site, the lookout spotted a single-funnelled vessel heading straight towards them. Presuming, quite rightly as it turned out, that it must be an Allied ship, the crew raised the Union Jack, upside down. Although this was the internationally recognised symbol of distress, the crew of *Anglo-Canadian* quickly scrambled to bring a large deck-mounted gun on the stern to life and aimed it at the defenceless boat. The captain then ordered them to come alongside.

Looking down upon the stricken vessel, one of the crewmen enquired, 'Where the hell have you come from?'

Lyon calmly replied, between deep puffs on his pipe, 'Just from Sumatra.'

The scramble nets were lowered and the crew of *Sederhana Djohanes* climbed aboard. The ship's captain was extremely concerned over possible enemy activity, especially the threat posed by submarines but, although he made it clear he was in a hurry to sail, he ordered *Sederhana Djohanes* to be scuttled, as the boat created a potential danger to Allied vessels leaving Columbo. Shells from the stern gun, manned by a merchant seaman, hit the frail and tired boat with surprising accuracy but *Sederhana Djohanes,* in a final act of defiance, refused to sink.

Lyon leaned over the stern rail in contemplative mood as the boat, its masts shattered, bravely stayed afloat. Like the rest of his comrades, he could not help but feel great affection and gratitude for the vessel that had delivered them all to safety, when so many others had died in the attempt. In the end, no one witnessed *Sederhana Djohanes'* final moments. When last seen, the stricken boat was bobbing away towards the horizon. However, over the coming days, as the adventurers regained their fitness and health, they shared tales of their incredible 52-day-long voyage of 1,700 nautical miles, in a boat designed for inshore and river sailing, certainly not to sail half-way across the Indian Ocean at the worst possible time of year. The perilous voyage was an experience they would never forget; a voyage from which Lyon had clearly emerged as a leader with great capabilities and deep inner strength. It also proved to Lyon that, like a chameleon, the right vessel could pass unnoticed in territory occupied by the enemy. His creative mind began to tease out details of his idea, spawned with Reynolds on the Indragiri River.

The irony was that their hasty retreat from Sumatra was premature, as the Japanese did not turn up at Padang for over a week and, had the Dutch not closed the port, many of the 900 British service personnel left behind could have escaped. Repeated offers by Colonel Warren, who was soon to become a prisoner of war, to go on the offensive to allow those who could still escape to do so, were rejected out of hand by the Dutch. Instead, all Allied soldiers were compulsorily disarmed and prevented from taking any small ships to escape, even though there were plenty of experienced Royal Navy personnel to crew them. In the interests of negotiating better surrender terms, there would be no resistance – something the Dutch would come to deeply regret, as all those captured faced more than three years of deprivation, and, in so many cases, death.

Colonel Warren was captured and taken to work on the infamous Burma-Thai Railway. For his work in instigating escape and evacuation of so many from Singapore, he was later awarded the Distinguished Service Order. He survived the war to become a schoolmaster, teaching English in Fairfax, Virginia, in the USA.

On board *Anglo-Canadian*, the crew of *Sederhana Djohanes* settled into unaccustomed and relative luxury. Lyon was summoned to the captain's cabin, where he was informed that their destination was to be the much safer port of Bombay, on the west coast of India. The voyage, of some 940 nautical miles, would take several days' sailing. Thanking the captain and bidding him goodnight, Lyon retired to his cabin, where his thoughts again turned to the indomitable Bill Reynolds. He wondered where his newfound friend could be, or if he were even still alive. Reynolds' final words as they had parted had been, 'If we both make it, we will meet again in India'.

As Lyon was to discover, his friend had indeed reached India. The voyage, which had lasted just 16 days, had ended at Nagapattinam, Reynolds' planned destination, a port on the southeast coast of India, not far from Madras. It was a feat of exceptional seamanship and navigation, accomplished without any charts and with only a basic compass to assist in his navigation.

Lyon eventually met up again with Reynolds in Bombay, where the Royal Indian Naval Dockyard were undertaking repairs on the ship that were beyond local mechanics at Nagapattinam. However, since Lyon had last seen the fishing boat there had been a name change. At the request of Reynolds' Chinese crew, *Kofuku Maru* had shed its Japanese origins and had been renamed The British Privateer *Suey Sin Fah*, a Chinese name meaning lotus flower, one that was far better 'joss', at the same time reflecting Reynolds' somewhat swashbuckling tendencies. Lyon also learned that, after he and Morris had gone on their way, Reynolds had continued to assist in rescue and relief work until the Japanese made it too hot to remain any longer, eventually rescuing 1519 castaways.

Lyon now appreciated even more the chameleon nature of Reynolds' ship. As *Kofuku Maru*, and then *Suey Sin Fah*, the little fishing boat had not only managed to escape Singapore but had then sailed back and forth between Sumatra and the islands, up and down the Indragiri River, to emerge unscathed. Furthermore, the vessel had made the passage unchallenged through the heavily patrolled and narrow Straits of Malacca.

The pair took time out to share their recent memories and cement their mutual respect. Who, but they, could appreciate the courage and inner strength shown by all those who had come through the maelstrom and carnage? Using their unique experience and knowledge, they now refined their plan to strike back at an enemy that had so ruthlessly captured so much of the free world in such a relatively short time.

Lyon's intimate knowledge of South-east Asian waters convinced him that no enemy could effectively control the oceans surrounding the Malay peninsula and Singapore. The myriad of islands, which he and Reynolds knew so well, along with their knowledge of the idiosyncrasies of the tides and currents, were essential to the success of their plan. However, to establish outsiders' confidence in an operation, which would undoubtedly be met with an almost incredulous disbelief by an orthodox military and naval hierarchy, would need very careful handling.

Lyon must influence some of the most senior Australian and British officials to gain tacit support for his plan. At the same time, he and Reynolds would need to develop strategy and logistics that could realistically, with the support of risk-averse leaders at the highest level, stand some small chance of success. This undertaking required a very special and singular type of leadership, as well as a loyal and like-minded group, who would be asked to pull off the seemingly impossible against a vastly superior enemy that had run rough shod over the British and Dutch Empires in the far east.

By March 1942, with just eleven divisions, Japan had secured a strategic victory, stretching from Hong Kong in the north, across the equator to the islands of Dutch East Indies and into the south-west Pacific. Military leaders worldwide were aghast at what is still considered to be one of the most successful military campaigns in history.

America had suffered the indignity of Pearl Harbour, whereupon Churchill had vowed to stand shoulder to shoulder with his American cousins. However, Britain's subsequent loss of Burma, Hong Kong, Malaya and Singapore were viewed with disquiet by the United States, who had become Churchill's key ally. The failure of the mother country, after so many promises, to protect her 'kith and kin' in Australia with the Far Eastern Fleet, had been very damaging.

To Ivan Lyon, the Japanese success and complete wresting of the British grip on South-east Asia was an anathema. Disillusioned by the lack of British military foresight, he was bewildered by the arrogance of the British to carry on with business as usual in Malaya and Singapore, thinking by doing so that the Japanese would be deterred from attacking. It had seemed plain enough to him that it was only a matter of time before the Japanese made their move.

Ever since his secondment from the Gordon Highlanders to SOE, Lyon had entered a world of unorthodox military procedure. His vision would challenge the conventional thinking of many in authority, but would also inspire others to train for a truly intrepid mission. To carry it out would take great courage and stealth. But first, he had to convince those in a position of power that his plans were quite frankly not those of a madman or someone who may be considered cavalier.

Lyon arrived at SOE headquarters in India like a 'whirling dervish'. Although Colin Mackenzie, spymaster and commander of SOE's Force 136 (as SOE India Mission was also known) was a gentleman in its truest sense, he was a typical manifestation of Churchill's Secret Army, responsible for executing war in Europe by ungentlemanly means. Mackenzie had lost a leg in World War I, but he had not let this perceived handicap affect his drive and enthusiasm. Highly intelligent, he had graduated with honours from Cambridge University and also served as a Director alongside Lord Linlithgow in J P Coates, an international cotton firm in Glasgow. Lord Linlithgow now held the highly influential position of Viceroy of India. As a personal friend of Mackenzie, he was to become the first and vital link in securing Lyon's future plans.

Through Mackenzie, Lyon was able to convince Lord Linlithgow that *Kofuku Maru* could infiltrate Japanese occupied waters to reach Singapore, where hand-picked and highly trained saboteurs could execute some serious damage against Japanese shipping and land installations. Lyon highlighted his knowledge of the islands and their mangrove swamps, which would provide ideal cover for hiding in daylight hours, prior to an attack.

At this stage, no decision had been made regarding the point from which the proposed operation would depart. It was initially thought it would be either India or Ceylon, and come under the control of Force 136. However, Mackenzie was aware that secrets were not easily kept on the Indian sub-continent. He also knew that SOE was setting up a covert organisation, Force 137, operating as SOE Australia. Operatives would be recruited to undertake secret and clandestine missions against the enemy, in and around occupied Japanese territories. Mackenzie convinced Lyon and Campbell that their proposed mission had a better chance of success if it were organised and embarked from Australia.

With ebullient enthusiasm, Lyon met again with Bill Reynolds. Over some well-earned Indian beers, Lyon almost overwhelmed him, as he outlined his latest plan. The laconic Australian heard him out, and his wry smile confirmed to Lyon that his faithful compatriot also thought that the plan, whilst astonishingly ambitious, was definitely doable.

With that settled, Lyon and Reynolds both agreed that the name *Suey Sin Fah*, chosen by Reynold's Chinese crew as a form of safeguard and blessing, was a bit lame for what the pair hoped to do. They needed something with a bit of bite to it. As Men of Empire, they had an appreciation of Rudyard Kipling and his books, set in India. In the story *Rikki Tikki Tavi*, the mongoose that took on deadly king cobras, Kipling introduced another snake as a character, the small but deadly krait, a reptile that abounds in South-east Asia. The krait warns, 'Be careful I am death, the dusty brown snaking that lies for choice on the dusty earth and his bite is as dangerous as a cobra's. But he is so small that nobody thinks of him and so he does more harm.' Although those destined to carry out one of the most daring missions behind enemy lines might not fully appreciate the meaning, or thought behind the name, the analogy was perfect.

For many decades there was a presumption that Jaywick, the name chosen by Lyon for the mission, was inspired by a small seaside town on the south-east coast of England. Blessed with an off-beat sense of humour, Lyon selected J-Wick, the name of a highly effective deodorizer made by Jeyes, an English sanitation company, and used in Singapore to remove highly noxious smells from the city's public lavatories.

Believing that they would depart from India, Bill Reynolds busied himself organising chandlers and suppliers, while the engineers in Bombay overhauled the weather beaten *Krait* and the engine, ready for the highly secret mission. However, Lyon now advised that the mission's team would train and embark from Australia. Lyon knew Reynolds was not one to turn down a challenge, but they both knew the voyage from India to Sydney would be highly perilous. With his usual disregard for danger, Reynolds immediately began charting a route through the largely enemy-controlled waters.

Lyon was an excellent judge of character and in the past months he had worked with three men who had the courage, character, and ability to help him plan and execute the attack. During their voyage from Sumatra to Ceylon, Lyon had shared many of his thoughts with Jock Campbell, who would be a great ally and advocate for Lyon and his plan. His maturity and experience in business and in managing people would also be invaluable. In Campbell, Lyon had a wise elder who had the ability to oil the cogs and assist him in persuading people that their proposal was not a pipe dream. Campbell was also an ideal behind-the-scenes factotum, with the strategic and tactical know-how to oversee the logistics, approvals, and effective delivery of the operation, the details of which were being evolved.

The second man, Bill Reynolds, was an indefatigable character, unquestioningly brave, cool headed in a crisis and with the necessary navigational experience. He also had his fishing boat, which he could sail where others feared to go. Lyon was about to track down the third man, when his personal life was turned upside down.

Just prior to Mackenzie's convincing Lyon that the proposed mission should take place from Australia, Lyon had made arrangements for Gabrielle and Clive to sail to India to join him. With the sudden change in plan, he had sent an urgent message telling Gabrielle to remain in Australia, but he was too late. Anxious to join him, she had taken the first available passage to India. He now learned that they were on board the SS *Nankin*, which had left Fremantle on 5 May and that all contact had been lost. The ship had disappeared without trace somewhere in the Indian Ocean, presumably sunk by a Japanese submarine or surface raider. It was considered that there was little chance of any survivors.

Those surrounding Lyon were hugely sympathetic to his terrible loss, offering help and solace. However, as a quiet and intensely private man, he found it hard to express or even show the deep emotions he was feeling. He simply blocked out his tragic news, channeling his grief into striking at the source of what had been a national humiliation, but which had just become deeply personal. To outsiders he may have appeared uncaring, cold-hearted even. Only those close to him knew the internal torture he was going through, believing he would never see his wife and child again.

Turning again to the task at hand, Lyon was able to add a third member to his team when the high command in Delhi approved a flight to Ceylon, so that he could meet a compatriot he had last seen in Padang – Ron Morris. Morris had already proven himself to be not only loyal and resolute, but highly dependable and a man who could turn his hand to almost anything. Most importantly, he had the ability to get things done. Always cheerful and positive, Lyon believed he would be an important member of the team.

Lyon's sole objective in travelling to Ceylon was to get Morris released from medical duties in the British Military Hospital, where life was far removed from the excitement and adventure he and Morris had experienced of late. However, his meeting with the Commanding Officer of 55 Military Hospital in Ceylon did not go well. Although Lyon spoke highly of Morris and recounted their exploits in escaping Singapore and ensuring safe passage to many hundreds of men, women and children, the CO was not impressed. He refused point blank to agree to Morris's release.

For once, Lyon had to admit a temporary defeat. Telling a highly disappointed Morris to keep in good cheer, Lyon flew back to Delhi. Determined to get his man, he went straight to the top, obtaining an official order sanctioning Morris's release, signed by General Wavell, Commander-in-Chief, India. Upon receipt of a copy of this weighty correspondence, Morris's CO reluctantly acquiesced. When Morris was summoned and given his orders to proceed to Australia, his delight in escaping his day-to-day duties was all too apparent to his Commanding Officer, who was clearly not amused.

Within days, Morris and Campbell boarded the troop ship *Athlone Castle,* a commandeered passenger liner that was returning the battle-hardened soldiers of 9 Australian Division from the Middle East to their beloved homeland. The fighting qualities of the longest-serving Australian division in frontline combat had been praised by both Britain's Field Marshall Montgomery and The Desert Fox, Germany's highly respected General Erwin Rommel.

Lyon arrived in Australia full of confidence, as his powers of persuasion extended to a letter of introduction from General Wavell to General Douglas MacArthur, Supreme Allied Commander, South-west Pacific Area (SWPA), whose headquarters were at that time in Melbourne. However, MacArthur and his staff were in no mood for British bright ideas. The loss of Hong Kong, Burma, Malaya, and Singapore had severely dented any confidence the Americans may have had in British military might in that region.

Because of the extraordinary Japanese military expansion in South-east Asia, MacArthur and his team of 14, known as the Bataan Gang, had been forced to hastily evacuate their headquarters in Corregidor, in the Philippines, on the direct order of United States' President, Franklin D Roosevelt. They narrowly escaped capture by fleeing in fast torpedo boats through rough seas occupied by the Japanese Navy. Arriving safely at Mindanao in the southern Philippines, they boarded two B17 aircraft bound for Australia. MacArthur then travelled by train to Melbourne where, on

21 March, he made his famous speech, 'I came through and I will return.'

The American team were highly cynical of the motives of the British South-east Asia Command, SEAC, and renamed it 'Save England's Asiatic Colonies'. MacArthur's priorities lay in the defence of New Guinea and the Solomon Islands, in the hope of protecting the vital supply routes between America and Australia.

With Japanese incursions expected almost immediately, steps were taken to improve surveillance by reinforcing the vital network of the Royal Australian Navy's coast watchers, scattered along 100 different posts in the islands to Australia's north. Staffed by skilled operatives and connected by tele-radios, using highly classified frequencies, they would become part of the Allied Intelligence Bureau, or AIB, financed by the British, Dutch, American and Australian governments and, like the fledgling SOE Australia, would come under MacArthur's direct command.

Chapter Five

Striking Back from Australia

At the same time as the Allied Intelligence Bureau was being established, members of SOE Far East had arrived in Australia from Singapore. Major Egerton Mott, soon to be Colonel, was an experienced Special Operations Commander who had accompanied General Wavell on a flight to Java, just prior to Singapore's fall. Mott, who had escaped from Java in a fishing boat, was picked up by the Royal Australian Navy, arriving in Fremantle on 10 March, the day after Java surrendered. After sending a message to London, he was instructed to make his way to Melbourne where MacArthur and his Bataan Gang were operating, to establish SOE Australia. Mott's office was in 'Airlie', a grim, secretive-looking, grey mansion, protected by a high wall, in the wealthy Melbourne suburb of Toorak. Also under its roof was the Allied Intelligence Bureau.

Along with Mott was his long-time colleague, Major Trappes-Lomax, who had been at 101 STS in Singapore. Lyon, Campbell and Morris, all former members of SOE Far East, were immediately recruited to the embryonic SOE Australia organisation, which, for security purposes, was known as Inter-Allied Services Department, or IASD, and quite often simply as ISD. Not surprisingly, Lyon found a sympathetic ear in Mott and Trappes-Lomax.

Armed with his personal letter of introduction from General Wavell, and detailed plans for Operation Jaywick, Lyon and Mott arranged to meet General MacArthur's right-hand man, General

Charles Willoughby, as SOE Australia was ultimately under US command, and therefore needed its support. Lyon and Mott were utterly dejected by Willoughby's response. The letter had no effect and, if anything, caused the American to recoil from such an outlandish and risky idea. Without faltering, Mott, who had great belief in Lyon and his small team, continued to lobby and seek support with the Australian military, including army chief, General Thomas Blamey, who made it quite clear that he was not interested. As a proponent of unconventional warfare, Mott could not understand the negative attitudes and what he saw as a lack of ambition to strike back. However, while many hearts and minds needed winning over, Lyon, Campbell, and Morris were cheered by the fact that SOE in London supported Jaywick, undoubtedly due to input by Mott and Trappes-Lomax, and had committed £3,000 pounds of the £11,000 required to launch the mission. In time of war, the cutting of red tape and the acquisition of such a substantial sum was most unusual, confirming SOE's desire to see Jaywick become reality. With the funds made available, Lyon charged Morris and Campbell to start spending some of it on the essential items to pump-prime the mission.

In his attempt to lobby and persuade, Lyon left no stone unturned. His elder sister Ann Gordon lived in Australia and was married to an Australian naval officer. When he asked Ann if she could recommend him to people who may be sympathetic to his cause and able to influence the progression of Jaywick, she suggested her friend Mrs Casey, a charming lady and mother of Richard, an aspiring politician who would become future External Affairs Minister, Governor General of Australia and a Lord of the Realm. As if by chance, Lyon – dressed in uniform – entered the Menzies Hotel, where he knew Mrs Casey was enjoying afternoon tea. Noticing Lyon, and admiring his stature and bearing, she asked to be introduced to the handsome young Gordon Highlander officer and, realising that he was Ann's brother, invited him to take tea with her. Lyon, well aware of Mrs Casey's connections, asked politely if she could arrange for an introduction to Lord Gowrie, the Governor General. Gowrie, a Victoria Cross recipient, had enjoyed an esteemed military career and Lyon believed that given the opportunity he would surely support such an endeavour. Lyon was astonished when Mrs Casey announced that Gowrie was coming to her house for dinner the following evening and invited Lyon to join them. Trying very hard to not look like the cat that had got the cream, he graciously accepted.

At dinner Gowrie listened carefully to Lyon's plans to strike back at Japan. Following this encounter, things started to move more swiftly. Lyon was asked to brief the Director of Naval Intelligence Commander, Rupert B M Long, who was 'MI6's man' in Australia, had direct links with both MI5 and MI6, and was therefore a vital key ally. He immediately realised Jaywick's potential and arranged a meeting with the naval chief, Admiral Sir Guy Royle. Royle made it clear to Lyon that he had been thoroughly briefed by Gowrie and Long and that their, and his approval, had led to the full support of the Australian Commonwealth Navy Board. The Board agreed to assist in recruiting personnel and to provide training facilities for Jaywick, dockyard facilities for *Krait* and any logistical support required, including the rental of a flat in Potts Point in Sydney to serve as Jaywick's command centre.

Lyon now needed to find a fifth member for the team, to act as his 2nd in Command, or 2IC. That someone must be exceptionally tough, fit, resilient, capable of taking over command when needed and knocking volunteers into shape. Lyon's brother-in-law recommended a lieutenant in the Royal Naval Reserve, Donald Davidson, who had connections to the intelligence services and MI6 and who had met Lyon briefly in Singapore. The son of an Anglican vicar, Davidson, was a deeply principled man of strong character and moral values, who had many of the key elements Lyon was looking for. He was currently working in Naval Intelligence in a desk job in Melbourne and was thoroughly bored.

The more Lyon learned about him, the more he liked. In his pursuit of adventure, Davidson had paddled a canoe for 1200 kilometres along the Chindwin River in Burma, through jungle heavily populated by tigers, which he often liked to stalk on his own, unarmed, for the sheer thrill. Fond of the open countryside and sailing, with a deep appreciation of Eastern culture, he also had a gentle side, and enjoyed collecting insects and butterflies. His extensive collection was eventually acquired and displayed in the Victoria and Albert Museum in London.

He had also worked in Queensland as a jackaroo, and for the Bombay Burma Trading Company, which had started out trading timber in Burma but now owned extensive tea plantations in India. Davidson's girlfriend of many years, Nancy, had been left heartbroken back in England while he set about his adventures. However in the mid-1930s, tired of his lack of commitment, she had set off to the Far East in pursuit of the one she loved. They were soon married and moved to Singapore.

At the outbreak of war, Davidson became a staff officer in the Royal Navy. After organising the evacuation of his wife and baby daughter, born in Singapore at around the same time as Clive, Lyon's son, he too made good his escape to Australia, where he ended up with his desk job in Melbourne.

Satisfied that Davidson was his man, Lyon set off with Morris and Campbell from the Potts Point flat to meet Jaywick's latest recruit, who was arriving from Melbourne by train at Sydney's Central railway station. Entering the platform, they spotted a tall, gangly character with his head sticking out from a window of the carriage, a broad smile on his face and a distinctive monocle in his right eye. As he alighted from the train, he tripped on the step, falling with a huge thud that sent the aristocratic monocle shooting across the platform. Retrieving it, Morris carefully cleaned the eyeglass with his handkerchief and handed it to the now deeply embarrassed and disconcerted owner. However, his undignified arrival was soon forgotten as Davidson was briefed about the proposed attack on the Japanese in Singapore, which Lyon was eager to deliver on 15 February 1943, the first anniversary of Singapore's surrender.

While in Singapore, Davidson had met Lorraine Stumm, an Australian reporter covering the progress of the war for London and Sydney magazines and who, Davidson suspected, had connections to MI6, which co-opted journalists covertly. She had taken the journalist job in Singapore where her husband, Harvey, who had volunteered to serve in the Royal Australian Air Force had been posted there. In her writing, she had been highly critical of the Governor of Singapore, Shenton Thomas and her determination to report what she saw almost had her deported, with 24-hours' notice. The allegation was that she had defamed the Governor, who was violently opposed to the 'Buy a bomber for Britain' scheme, accusing him of failing to prepare the local population and military for an impending invasion.

Whilst the military leaders in Singapore had been in a high state of denial, many including Davidson were working on the assumption that total capitulation was inevitable. Moving in these circles, Stumm had become aware of the futility of the situation and through her articles was effectively communicating this to both London and Australia, where the Fairfax Press, which published a range of journals and newspapers in Australia and New Zealand, had known links to MI6.

Stumm's work had continued uninterrupted until 1800 hours on 22 June 1941, when she was admitted to Singapore General Hospital to give birth to her daughter Sheridan, at one minute past midnight. Almost six months later, in the early hours of 8 December, Stumm was crouching beneath an air raid shelter, Sheridan in her arms, sheltering from the first bombs dropped on Singapore. The day after the air raid, Stumm received a telegram from the editor of London's *Daily Mirror*, a previous employer, 'Delighted to know you are safe, can you become our accredited war correspondent and start filing stories immediately?' Stumm seized the opportunity to take an active part in the war effort and rushed to obtain her official documentation as a war correspondent. Early in 1942, however, she decided that the time had come to take her daughter to Australia and resigned her post. Back home, she wrote a number of retrospective pieces illustrating the pre-war situation in Singapore now fallen to the Japanese.

In August of that year, she contacted her London office with regard to some outstanding payments and was elated by the reply, 'All delighted you are safe. Money following. Can you represent us at General MacArthur's HQ in Brisbane?' Not one to refuse another golden opportunity, Stumm obtained reaccreditation under the Australian licence system, to become the only woman correspondent based at General MacArthur's headquarters. She built a good relationship with MacArthur, who had such confidence in her ability that he later officially endorsed her as the first Australian war correspondent to report from the battlefield in an American attack on the Japanese occupied city of Rabaul in Papua New Guinea. MacArthur's action deeply annoyed the Australian high command, which had banned women from taking part in such hazardous pursuits.

MacArthur's family were accommodated in three suites on the fourth floor of the historic and beautiful Lennon's Hotel in Brisbane, which the general codenamed 'Bataan', after the peninsula in the Philippines from where he had escaped. It is perhaps no coincidence that Davidson's previous relationship with Lorraine Stumm and her connection with MI6 played an important role in influencing the American high command. This in turn led to the supply of intelligence to Davidson and Lyon, even though Willoughby had made it clear American interests did not lie in Singapore. Lyon knew from the outset that MacArthur did not have a high regard for the British, and that as Supreme Commander, South-west Pacific Area (SWPA), he could have put a stop to Jaywick, if he so chose.

Lyon, ever the lone wolf, set off in search of a secret location, well out of the way of prying eyes, to be known as Camp X, where the operatives could train and bond. He decided on a location above a 30-metre-high cliff in a remote area of a national park to Sydney's north. It was above Refuge Bay, an inlet of Broken Bay, into which flowed the mighty Hawkesbury River.

Back in Sydney, in the Potts Point flat, Campbell and Morris were working with another member of the team, also vital to the success of Jaywick. She was Bettina Reid, granddaughter of Australia's first Prime Minister, Edmund Barton. Her husband had been taken prisoner of war by the Germans and, like Lyon, she had a deep desire and motivation to be part of something that would strike back hard against the enemy. Reid, who was secretary to the head of Military Intelligence, had the necessary security clearance and skills to become the mission's secretary, Lyon's Personal Assistant and to act as a quasi intelligence officer. As such, she was privy to all of Jaywick's plans, was present at all planning meetings and typed all the reports.

While Lyon had been away finding a suitable location for Camp X, Morris, Campbell, and Reid had set about organising their Potts Point office, a roomy apartment in Onslow Gardens, overlooking Sydney Harbour and not far from Naval Headquarters at Garden Island. SOE in London, backing Jaywick one hundred per cent, had now totally underwritten the £11,000 needed for the operation, the first instalment of which had been transferred to a secret account opened by Lyon in the Bank of New South Wales at its nearby Kings Cross branch.

In late September, Lyon flew to London for discussions with SOE. He also met with his parents and over dinner warned them that dangers lay ahead. His father, being a military man, admired his son's determination and courage, although neither he nor his wife were given any further details. All that Ivan could impart was that the fall of Singapore and the loss of Malaya had made him very angry and that he could be away for many months.

Meanwhile Davidson was tasked with finding 20 tough and resilient individuals capable of being trained for the secret mission. He interviewed 40 volunteers from Flinders Naval Depot, HMAS *Cerberus* in Victoria, and selected 20. Of these, only one had actually been to sea – Able Seaman Arthur Jones. They had all volunteered blindly with no idea what was in store or being planned.

While Davidson organised some basic training at the Naval Depot, Morris, along with Jaywick's cook, Allan Hobbs, and Leading Seaman Johnson, who was on loan for a limited period, set up Camp X on Broken Bay, where the shortlisted operatives were to be trained.

Their first task was to clear the ground of thick scrub and undergrowth, before tents could be erected to accommodate the trainees and instructional staff. A small stream ran through the camp, plunging over the cliff and into the cove below. The only connection with the outside world from this highly secret location was via *Ann*, a small dinghy, equipped with an outboard engine to provide transport to and from a jetty about six kilometres away at Coal and Candle Creek, another inlet of the Hawkesbury River. On reaching the beach at Refuge Bay, access to the camp was up a rope ladder slung over the edge of the cliff. In this deeply isolated location, Morris, Hobbs and Johnson set about cutting back the dense bush and undergrowth by hand and erecting tents. It was hard work. The camp was only partially ready by the time Davidson returned from Melbourne, to lend a hand to get it into shape before the recruits arrived on 6 September.

Camp X Refuge Bay

Morris, who had high standards and was a good judge of character, had confidence in both Jaywick's commanding officer and his 2IC. He admired and respected Lyon for his natural leadership skills, while Davidson had the ability and expertise to build a unique and deadly team. His great strength was that, like Lyon, he always led from the front and did not expect anyone to do anything he was not willing to do himself. When clearing the bush for the camp site with parangs, Morris was impressed that Davidson was able to keep up with him stroke for stroke. From the moment Morris first set eyes on Davidson, he realised that the innocuous monocle was an amiable affectation and that the 2IC was, like Lyon, a tough, reliable and trustworthy individual. Collectively, they had all the characteristics and individual skill sets to give the mission the very best chance of success. If the attack failed, they would also have the fortitude and know-how to survive and attempt an escape back to Allied lines.

Krait was expected to arrive in November. Lyon and Davidson were highly motivated to carry out the mission on 15 February 1943, the first anniversary of Singapore's fall. Allowing time to sail to the target area and prepare, this gave Davidson less than three months to finely hone his volunteer sailors into a single-minded force.

The first stage of the training had already taken place at the Army Physical and Recreational Training School in Frankston, on Victoria's Morning Peninsula, not far from the Naval Depot. It was said that the Army instructors, when dealing with naval recruits, were exceptionally brutal. However, after three very intensive weeks aimed to break the best of them, the 16 who passed muster were still very keen to continue – for what, they didn't know.

When the recruits arrived at Camp X, Davidson began training in earnest. The 16 hand-picked sailors were very enthusiastic and willing. Davidson was aware that they were very young, ranging from 17 to early twenties, but he needed them to be keen and flexible. Unlike normal service training where they must do as they were told, Davidson was intent on making them self-reliant, to eliminate what he termed 'second fiddle' complex.

Having survived an extremely tough and demanding selection process, the trainees were considered to have great potential. Both Lyon and Davidson set incredibly high standards in regard to character, physical strength, and mental agility as these men would have to gel to become a team, and hopefully survive, in extremely dangerous conditions, far behind enemy lines. To do this, Davidson planned to bring the team to a peak of physical condition and endurance. In his estimation, if all did not go to plan, they might need to spend six months behind Japanese lines, evading the enemy and making good their escape.

Neither Morris, Hobbs nor any of the recruits had any idea where they were going, or how they were to get there. They knew only that the actual mission involved paddling small two-man kayaks, known as folboats, to a target area where, under cover of darkness, they were to attach magnet limpet mines to the hulls of enemy ships.

The success of the whole mission rested on these young men and the distances they had to cover required supreme fitness and psychological strength. Newly designed folboats that had been trialed in the UK were found to be the best at handling rough seas and were fast and manoeuvrable. However, until the latest design arrived from England, they would have to make do with those currently available.

The folboats could be dismantled, put into a pack and carried using shoulder posts. Crews even practised scaling cliffs with the pack, using a specially designed head strap. As the small, rubberised canvas folboats were constantly in need of maintenance, the crews had to be highly proficient in repairing and preventing damage, and thoroughly cleaning the craft after use. Davidson also experimented with various coloured paints to camouflage the canoes, even under searchlight. Battleship grey, which was in plentiful supply, showed up at night far less than the natural folboat colour, army green but, in the end, black was deemed to be best for a night-time raid.

Training took place each day, up to 18 hours a day. Davidson supervised much of it, but weapon's training and demolition was left to specialist instructors.

Crews were repetitively put to the test by paddling out into the open sea at night and silently launching their small craft from beaches in Broken Bay in all weathers. Being able to paddle noiselessly and at full speed was absolutely essential, and was a very difficult skill to master. They had to practise how to recover from a capsize with a folboat heavily laden with limpet mines and other equipment. In a normal sea the folboat was capable of four knots.

While all crew members were trained to an exceptional standard, those designated as the attack party had intensive instruction on how to place limpet mines onto the hulls of ship, from a folboat, an exacting and demanding task. As the name suggests, a limpet was designed to 'cling on' using the world's most powerful magnet, and was the latest destructive naval technology, developed in 1938 by Military Intelligence Research in England for SOE. The magnet, developed in the laboratories of General Electric Company in New York and less than the size of an eraser, could attach an explosive charge to a metal hull or armoured tank. Each of the limpet mines used for Operation Jaywick had two magnets set in self-levelling sockets, on either side of the explosives chamber.

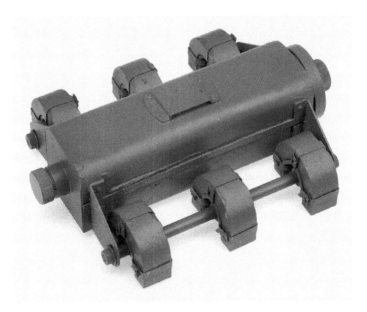

Deadly limpet mine

Each folboat party would need to carry nine limpet mines, three per ship, with each set weighing more than 45 kilograms. The interlinked mines, placed about two metres below the water level, were powerful enough to blow three large holes in the hulls of the targeted ships. The best means of approach was found to be from the windward side, allowing the breeze and flow of the water to hold the folboat against the vessel. With one operative using a magnetic pole to keep the folboat steady against the side of the ship, the other manoeuvred a wooden pole to lower the mine down the side of the vessel. Once the mine was in place and the fuse set, the folboat was allowed to drift to the end of the fuse line and place the second mine.

This extremely complex procedure had to be executed in the dark of night, so the teams practised repeatedly to refine the technique and to set the chemical fuses, which could be timed to detonate up to two days after placement. The more they practised, the more confident they became in undertaking a task for which no training manual had been written. By the end of the training period, crews could place two sets of mines and set the fuses in just under 20 minutes. For their final test, they carried out mock attacks on naval ships moored in the bay, without being detected, even though an 'attack' was expected and a close watch maintained.

Besides learning how to place limpet mines on ships, each recruit was required to paddle a folboat for long distances to reach and exit the target zone. As fitness improved, so did the distance to be paddled each day. The teams were also drilled hard on carrying out overland covert operations. The terrain around the camp, covered in dense undergrowth, was ideal for conditioning the men on what they might find on the isolated islands around Singapore, with which Lyon and Morris were so familiar. They were taught how to expertly stalk through such terrain, moving so silently that they covered only one kilometre in one hour. Much of the work was done barefoot, and Morris recorded that by the end of the training period their feet were so tough they could walk on razor-sharp coral. Exercises devised by Davidson saw them away from the camp for up to five days in loaded canoes, hiding by day and moving silently through the night.

Specialist instructors were brought to the camp to ensure the men were capable of handling a multiplicity of weapons, including the .303 Lee Enfield rifle, Owen sub-machine gun, Lewis machine gun, Bren gun, three-inch mortars, the German Luger revolver and Mills fragmentation grenades. In addition, each person had to demonstrate competence in semaphore and Morse Code, naval chart and map reading using both a compass and tide tables, as well as the ability to navigate by dead reckoning. Great emphasis was placed on not just the physical aspects of training, but also the psychological demands of being under constant threat, deep in enemy territory.

They also received training on how to attack and demolish land-based defensive and searchlight positions. This involved skills in the handling of dynamite and nitro-glycerine and competence in the many methods of sabotage. Demolition training was in the hands of newly recruited Sub Lieutenant Bert Overell, the camp's fitness instructor and an explosives expert, who set about his training program with great enthusiasm. Adding to his significant capability was a very tough British Army Major, Francis Chester. Born in South Africa to British parents, he was educated in a private boarding school in England, before entering Sandhurst Military College. On graduation, he served in King Edward Horse Cavalry Regiment, which had formed on the outset of World War I and had seen action in Ypres and on the Somme. After the war, Chester had managed a rubber plantation in Borneo but rejoined the army on the outbreak of war. He saw action this time round in Abyssinia and in May 1942 went to India, where he was recruited to SOE there and met Lyon. After serving with SOE in Burma, Chester joined SOE Australia at Lyon's request. Fluent in Malay and trained in internal sabotage and propaganda, Chester was perfect for Jaywick.

Chapter Six

Fine Tuning

Although many of those in High Command who had knowledge of Lyon's secret mission thought it was insane or even impossible, he knew that his crew members were trained in a way that no other member of the armed forces had been trained in the past. There were essentially two separate parts of the mission, to attack the ships in harbour, and for *Krait* to effectively maintain stealth until it was time to pick up the raiding party, a task equally important and extremely dangerous.

Morris undertook folboat and weapons training, but he, Hobbs and Sharples, the telegraphist/wireless operator, were not required to take part in the attack elements. However, drills were carried out to test the team's response, should *Krait* come under attack or if the enemy made an attempt to board.

Lyon and Davidson had many conversations about the mission and wrestled with the idea of telling the Jaywick team where they were heading, thinking perhaps that this would better prepare them for the magnitude of what they were attempting. However, in the end they decided that it was just too risky to tell anyone, other than those who needed to know, as a leak could prove to be catastrophic.

The training was constant and was deemed ferocious. Davidson was determined to train his volunteers to a level that would ensure the very best chance of survival, in what would be the longest behind-the-lines sabotage mission ever attempted. He was concerned about maintaining morale, as the men had no idea where they were heading, and keeping them interested as the training progressed was demanding. He knew that discipline alone was not the answer. Training to such a high standard was essential but, to survive the cull, personal motivation and the character of an individual were paramount.

Davidson and Lyon both led by example, everything was always demonstrated first by them. This included handling folboats in dangerous seas; endurance tests, paddling and carrying folboats overland for long distances; fighting and self-defence using knives; competence in the use of all weapons; unarmed and silent killing and, indeed, every facet of the mission, small and large, even down to eating the dehydrated rations.

While in the camp, the men ate two hearty meals a day, morning and evening, cooked over an open fire, for which they were expected to chop the wood. 'Lights out' were at 2200 hours sharp, and everyone invariably fell asleep immediately, such was the extent of the daily exertions.

A welcome and enjoyable respite was what Davidson term as 'Erudition' sessions. Morris, who was famed for his vocabulary, was consulted over its meaning. The sessions were conducted under canvas in a makeshift classroom and the crew listened carefully, trying to pick up a hint of where they were heading, as Davidson and Lyon explained the customs of local people they may need to come to rely on – the body language that would endear them to those they met, and that which may offend, as well as the precautions needed to minimise contracting diseases.

Lyon and Davidson were always very careful not to mention any specific locations. However one day Morris, who listened intently, felt a shudder go down his spine as Lyon demonstrated with Davidson how to approach a native who might be sympathetic and give them shelter or food. He had seen Lyon do this on a number of occasions on the islands around Singapore when they had been setting up food dumps ready for the evacuation. *Surely*, he thought, *they wouldn't risk going back to Singapore, which was now at the very heart of the newly established Japanese Imperial*

Empire? This was something he kept very much to himself and gave him more than one sleepless night.

Davidson and the instructors understood that they had to build each individual's mental resilience. Living conditions on the voyage would be extremely confined and crew members on a 70-foot long boat had to get on. They would sail in tropical monsoons, through hazardous waters, in daylight and under cover of darkness. The only contact with the outside world would be in the case of an extreme emergency and, even then, requesting help would be both futile and foolhardy. As Lyon well knew, breaking radio silence behind enemy lines was akin to an act of suicide, so very strict protocols had been put in place.

As the days passed, strong friendships were forged, but Davidson watched carefully for any sign of disharmony or egotism, neither of which would be tolerated, as unified teamwork was vital to the mission. He inflicted tough love, but he commanded the highest level of respect from all of those in Camp X. He was also relentless with his training schedule, but the sailors knew that they could be called upon to put their knowledge and training into practice, once the mission was actually underway. Davidson was exceptionally good at selecting the right people for the job and determining who would be able to cope with the mental and physical challenges that lay ahead. Davidson, with Overell's help, had the unenviable task of whittling down the numbers to form the final select group.

Besides the three officers, one person who was automatically included was Ron Morris. In Morris, Lyon knew that he had a loyal and very able ally. At Refuge Bay he was in charge of the camp and its efficient running, while supporting Jock Campbell with the complex logistics necessary to embark on such a hazardous undertaking. Lyon also knew that Morris had the ability to enhance the smooth running of the mission across a broad range, not the least of which was maintaining good morale. As a member of SOE Australia he was also able to hone his skills in combat and sabotage. Had he simply have been 'attached' to the organisation, he would have remained on the war establishment of his parent unit, the RAMC, as a non-combatant. The distinction allowed him to be released from the constraints of the Royal Army Medical Corps and of the Geneva Convention, which stated 'medics can only use force in self defence of their own lives or those in their care'.

When setting up the camp, Morris had decided that an incinerator was needed to burn items that may, if discovered, give away highly sensitive details regarding the team or the planned missions objectives. The chances of discovery were not high, but their presence was known to an army outpost, perched high on the cliffs at Commodore Heights, guarding the entrance to the Hawkesbury River. Taffy, as Morris had been dubbed, discovered a steep fissure in the rock face behind the camp, where he could light a fire, with a narrow crevice acting as a chimney. As the camp needed a latrine, he decided that the rock fissure could serve as a drop-through pit, with any solid waste burnt in the make-shift incinerator below, along with the rubbish and any documents that needed to be destroyed. After fixing a toilet seat to two planks straddling the gap, he stood back to admire his handy work.

Always the early riser, Morris thought he would trial his new invention while the remainder of the camp was still asleep. However, the fire failed to burn as brightly as he hoped, so he collected a can of kerosene from the fuel store. Although he had checked initially that no one was sitting on the toilet above, Freddie Marsh, who had woken with a 'gippy' stomach – food poisoning – was now in occupation. Down below, oblivious that anyone was in residence, Morris poked at the fire, causing small flames to flicker. He then doused the burning embers with a generous application of kerosene, to truly test the chimney and the effectiveness of his innovative incinerator. At first, nothing happened. Then, as the flammable liquid vaporised, there was a violent explosion and flames shot up the chimney.

Luckily, Marsh had felt a surge of heat and pressure split seconds before the flames arrived. 'What the f**k was that?' he screamed, while performing a war dance on the top of the rock. He was definitely not amused but Morris, ever the practical joker, thought this was hilarious and never did admit, not even to himself, that he could have caused poor Marsh irreparable damage. After this incident, it became standard practice for those using the facilities topside to shout a warning down the crevice, threatening Morris with a long, slow and painful death should he light the fire while they went about their business.

One of Morris's other tasks was to take the dinghy to Coal and Candle Creek to collect supplies delivered by Bettina Reid. On his return, like all other Jaywick members, he had to scale the cliff using the rope ladder. This time, however, he had a substantial bag of rations. Clambering up the 30-metre cliff-face on a swaying rope ladder was never easy, but the rations made it almost impossible. Usually, Morris would have shouted for a rope to be thrown down to haul them aloft but, on this occasion, everyone seemed to have disappeared from the camp. As he struggled to just past halfway, cussing and sweating profusely and getting more and more frustrated at his slow progress, he came face-to-face with an extremely large lizard which, unlike Morris, seemed to be enjoying the sun.

It was a case of head-to-head combat, for which Morris was ill-equipped. At 20 metres above the rocky beach and just 30 centimetres from the fearsome monster's head, he knew that if the creature challenged him he would fall to his death. As the lizard's forked tongue shot out, Morris focused his steely eyes on his adversary with what he hoped was an intimidating stare and said, 'Now, my friend, we are not going to hurt each other, are we?', wondering at the same time who was the most frightened. Morris held his gaze. The prehistoric-looking reptile hissed loudly and decamped, scuttling up and over the rocks with speed and agility that Morris truly admired.

The lizard was a lace monitor, one of 27 species of monitors found in Australia, which varied in length from 20 centimetres to more than two metres. Although Morris thought it was a giant iguana, he was not that far off the mark as monitors are also known as goannas in Australia, a corruption of 'iguana', the name given to them by early colonists.

Throughout the training period, Lyon remained a distant character, carefully watching over Davidson and the team. He was the strategic brain, with all the right skills and in command of operatives who were expected to achieve something remarkable. The odds of success were very slim, and Lyon knew this.

After careful culling by Davidson, Lyon announced the names of the eight men who had made the cut. However, this list would later be reduced to five. The first three, Arthur Jones, Walter Falls and Andrew Huston, along with three officers, would be part of the final attack crew, with Mostyn Berryman and Frederick Marsh in reserve. They formed the operational team. Morris and the cook, along with *Krait*'s crew, would bring the final total to 14. Davidson and Lyon privately knew they had chosen well. Their affectionate term for the operational team was 'a young and happy-go-lucky bunch of thugs'.

There was Arthur Jones, known as Arty, a very serious individual who, unlike many others, did not have the greatest sense of humour. He was the only sailor who had been to sea – on the RAN's cruiser *Manoora*. The constant exposure to the sun and elements had given his skin a deeply tanned appearance, which, with his slim build, meant he could easily be mistaken for an Asian.

Walter Falls, known variously as Wally or Poppa, was the father figure, being the eldest at 23 years old. He had a heavy muscular build, was very intelligent, and deemed to be very good looking. His calmness and reliability was infectious, and Davidson noticed he had a very positive effect on the younger members of the crew.

Andrew Huston, aged just 17, was ironically nicknamed Happy as he rarely smiled. However, during training he had shown great fortitude and mental strength for one so young. He, like Jones, tanned easily and could be mistaken as a native of the region in which they were to sail. He showed a commitment and willingness to learn new skills, which Davidson thought was driven by the desire to keep up with the slightly older members of the crew.

Frederick Marsh (Boof), Huston's best friend, was exceptionally good with his hands. As an ex-cabinet maker, he quickly grasped weapons' handling and the tying of knots and lines. He had intelligent eyes, was agile, good at sport, a natural team player and an all-round, reliable 'good egg'. A deadly fighter with a knife or garrote, or even with his bare hands, Marsh was capable of committing extreme and clinical violence against an enemy. However, he also demonstrated a calmness and sociability that blended him into the team.

The fifth member was Mostyn Berryman, or Moss, a quiet young man with almost chameleon tendencies, who was like a sponge, soaking up knowledge and skills that would help him to kill and survive. Although he was only 19, he would go on to be an extremely solid member of the crew.

Like Lyon, Morris had a degree of mystique about him. A very humble, unshakable and reliable man, as well as a highly skilled first aider, he had already proven his all-round ability in the field of action. Although the Australian members of the crew had great difficulty in deciphering his Welsh accent, Morris instilled calm in those around him.

By this time, word of the success of the trial attacks and the skill of the Jaywick operatives had filtered through to the top brass and it was not by accident, but by design. Lyon needed to keep the confidence of many stakeholders, including the American Commanders in the Pacific, especially General MacArthur who, if he so chose, could scupper Jaywick with a single command. Ever the tactician, Lyon had set up a network via back channels so that a steady flow of news of their successes in training would reach MacArthur's HQ, ensuring that confidence was maintained.

Morris was delighted one morning when Lyon beckoned him and asked him to undertake a very extraordinary duty. The camp was to have a special guest. That morning, Lyon had been contacted by radio and told to expect none other than Lord Gowrie, Governor General of Australia. Sensing that this was a positive sign that Jaywick was definitely on, Lyon briefed camp members on the importance of such a high-level visit and the need to instil confidence at the highest level of influence.

Turning to Morris he said, 'Taffy, I want you to use all your charm on this visit. We are to have a gentleman who has it in his power to see us succeed or fail in our endeavours. It would be a shame, my friend, if all our efforts since we escaped from Singapore were not to be given the very best chance of success.'

Morris was aware of Gowrie and of his reputation amongst Australians. He had arrived in Australia from England in the mid-1920s, during the Great Depression, to take up an appointment as Governor of South Australia. His handling of the extremely unstable political situation at that time had earned him a level of respect not normally enjoyed by British officials. As a major in the Welsh Guards from April 1915, he had fought gallantly at Gallipoli and was severely wounded at Suvla Bay in August, before serving in France. This war record also made him deeply respected – unlike Winston Churchill, for whom Australians had exceptionally strong feelings over the sacrifice of ANZAC Forces during the Gallipoli landings. His mishandling of the situation in Singapore a generation later had led to the feeling that history had repeated itself.

Lyon and Morris discussed their concerns that Camp X had no jetty to disembark such a senior visiting official. Up until now, visitors either got their feet wet or jumped out of a boat and scrambled across the rocks. Building a jetty was not possible within the timescale and would have attracted unwanted attention to the camp. Neither Lyon nor Morris had ever envisaged entertaining such a distinguished guest. What could they do?

The ever practical Morris said, 'I will carry him ashore, because we can't see him get his feet wet, now, can we?'

Lyon liked the suggestion, but they agonised over how to get their VIP up to the camp. Lyon's insistence in using the ladder to make the ascent up the cliff was iron-clad but, in this case, rules had to be eased, as the Governor General – although sprightly – was in his early 60s. The pair put together a plan. Morris's feet were so hardened that he would wade out over the rocks and and give Lord Gowrie a piggyback. They knew that Gowrie would enjoy this escapade and hopefully find it amusing. For the final part of his journey to Camp X he would be hauled to the top of the cliff in a bosun's chair.

On 5 December the Governor General arrived, with little pomp and no circumstance. Morris signalled the small launch to come to a halt some 30 metres from shore to prevent the propeller from grounding in the shallow water. Morris noticed that Gowrie, who was in uniform, was wearing, along with many other honours, the Victoria Cross ribbon that he had won in the Sudan campaign in 1898 for rescuing a badly injured Egyptian soldier. He also noted the perplexed look on the faces of Gowrie and the sailor at the tiller, as they wondered how they were expected to come ashore, especially the Governor General, dressed in his best uniform.

With that, Morris waded out in a dramatic fashion, shouting, 'Wait there, sir, I will be carrying you ashore.' To which Gowrie remarked, 'This should be interesting.'

'Would you be good enough to climb on my back, sir?' invited Morris, in his broad and almost undecipherable Welsh accent.

Putting absolute faith in the tough and robust ex-coalminer, Gowrie clung to Morris' back like one of the limpet mines with which the men had practised so many times. Lyon, Davidson, and the instructors looked on with a mixture of amusement and fear, lest Morris drop or flounder with the Governor General on his back. However, the sure and steady Welshman reached the shore without mishap and lowered Gowrie slowly onto *terra firma*.

Gowrie turned and, with a wry smile, said, 'Which part of Scotland do you come from, Taffy?'

The visit was a huge success, with the men carrying out a range of displays, carefully orchestrated to show off their skills. Unlike the majority of the members of Camp X, Gowrie knew where they were heading. It was just as well that they did not realise that their Vice-Regal visitor was making a critical analysis of their capabilities, and that he would have no hesitation in pulling the plug on Jaywick, should he feel that he was sending men to their deaths.

His final act before taking his leave was to launch a vessel from the beach, a two-man experimental kayak built by Davidson and Marsh from plywood and reclaimed timber, a task designed to both test ingenuity and to help crew members to see that, if necessary, they could build their own craft in an emergency. Its name was painted neatly on the bow – HMAS *Lyon*.

HMAS Lyon at Camp X

Entering into the spirit of things, Gowrie ceremoniously proclaimed, 'I name this ship HMAS *Lyon,* and may the Lord protect her and all who sail in her.' He was also one of the few standing on the beach who realised that the Jaywick team would need many such blessings to have a chance of success. Back on his launch, Gowrie said to the sailor on the tiller, 'You know, I think they may just succeed.' Without a clue of what the Governor General was on about, the sailor replied, 'Yes, sir.'

Meanwhile, Jock Campbell had been having a torrid time trying to get *Krait* from India to Australia, poor Bill Reynolds having failed, through engine troubles, to get it ready in time to sail it himself. *Krait* had needed a much bigger refit than was first thought and, with time running out, she was eventually shipped to deck cargo MV *Shillong*, a 5,000-ton, armed merchantman.

Campbell had been so concerned about *Krait* and the delay that he had taken the precaution of sourcing other vessels that could be used, such as luggers or trawlers. However, the news that *Krait* had departed from Bombay on 29 November and would arrive in Sydney by late December certainly raised morale in the camp. Neither Lyon nor Morris, who knew *Krait* intimately, had said anything about the small fishing boat to the others, so each member of the crew had his own mental picture of the mystery vessel that was to take them to some indeterminate place, where they could put their newfound skills to use.

For the Christmas of 1942, Morris remained in the camp while the rest took some well-earned leave to meet loved ones and have a few beers. However, Morris received a special present, when he learned that *Krait* had arrived in Sydney Harbour on Christmas Day, which also happened to be his birthday. However, there *Krait* remained, as the docks were dead and would not spring into life until the New Year celebrations were over.

This torturous delay further threatened Lyon's timetable of an attack date of 15 February. Festive dock workers, having finished welcoming the New Year of 1943, finally returned to work on 2 January to crane *Krait* off the deck of *Shillong,* which tragically, three months later would be torpedoed by a German submarine with a loss of 72 lives.

In the process of lifting *Krait* from the freighter's deck, damage was sustained to the small fishing boat's hull, which meant more days wasted while repairs were made. While life went on as usual in the camp, Campbell, Davidson, and Lyon were by this point feeling a little distraught. Having invested great time and energy in the crew and knowing their state of readiness, it would be intolerable if they did not have *Krait* fit and seaworthy to make the journey.

In the camp, with such uncertainty, much was done to try and keep morale high. The intensity of the training did not abate but, as a treat, the team were allowed to paddle across to the small bayside village of Patonga, on the Hawkesbury estuary, some 16 kilometres across the water from Refuge Bay. Protected from the southerly swells, Patonga had a small sandy beach, a post office, a general store, some holiday shacks and a netted area to protect swimmers from sharks, as the waters near the mouth of the river were a favourite haunt of the ocean's top predator.

The local community was welcoming, and the fun-loving crew members undoubtedly enjoyed the company of equally fun-loving young ladies, who had escaped Sydney to enjoy the sun and were fascinated by the unexpected influx of fit, tanned, young men. The beer was also an attraction. The visitors did not over indulge, though, as they knew the return journey in the dark was hazardous, and they did not want to keep the sharks company in the water. When the men swam in the bay at Camp X, a sentry always kept watch for sharks from the cliff top, armed with a Bren gun. However, should the boat turn turtle out in the middle of the bay there was no such protection.

One evening when the others were visiting Patonga, Marsh, who had remained behind at the camp, placed a freshly killed snake (not uncommon around the camp) into Falls'camp bed. When Falls returned, Marsh lay on his stretcher, almost in tears, trying not to laugh as his friend undressed and climbed under the blanket. Unbelievably, there was no reaction. Within minutes, all he could hear was Falls snoring deeply. At four in the morning, the entire camp was woken by a blood-curdling scream. Falls stomped around the camp, shouting expletives and threatening the most horrible and slow death to the perpetrator. He never did find out who it was, and Marsh never told anyone.

The camp had also attracted a feline friend – a beautiful white Persian cat, which the crew named Cleopatra. One night, the neat and tidy Morris, who had carefully laid out his pyjamas on his camp bed, came into his tent to find four gorgeous newborn kittens lying on them. The men decided to keep Cleopatra and the kittens were gifted as mascots to the Australian naval vessels that the attack team had been using as targets during training exercises.

With the delay in the arrival of *Krait,* Campbell laid down the gauntlet to the Commander of the army gun battery at Commodore Heights. The establishment was manned and protected by 200 gunners, and watch was kept 24 hours a day. The Jaywick team was charged with taking over the entire battery, which was put on high alert and instructed that it could be attacked.

Morris and another member of the crew set off first, paddling a folboat stealthily along the estuary and landing about three kilometres from their objective, the battery's perimeter, protected by heavy Lewis machine guns set 50 metres apart. Undetected, the pair crawled up gullies dug for drainage to a point where Morris could hear the Commander firmly instructing his personnel that an attack from commandoes could be imminent, before heading off to another part of the camp to repeat the message. As soon as he was out of sight, Morris slid silently down the bank and, emerging from the undergrowth, pressed the hard muzzle of a German Luger into the spinal cord of the sentry. Needless to say, he surrendered immediately and was roughly bound and gagged. Morris then used the field telephone at the machine-gun post to contact the next gun emplacement. Assuming an Australian accent he drawled, 'Hey, mate, can you come over and give me a hand? I think we could be going to be attacked.' As soon as he arrived, the second gunner surrendered and met the same fate.

Shortly afterwards, the remaining Jaywick members struck six other key perimeter locations with equal success. Intercepting a lorry carrying rations along the only access road, they ordered the driver and his mate to undress at gunpoint, then gagged and tied them up. Now dressed in their clothes, two of the raiders, with the rest of their comrades hidden in the rear, drove through the compound gates unchallenged and up to the guardhouse. Swiftly overcoming the guards, they took over the battery's telephone exchange and, sending false messages to each outpost, created enough chaos to allow them to take all 200 personnel without firing one shot. Not surprisingly, in due course news of the success of the raid at Commodore Heights found its way to the High Command, through Lyon's channels of communication.

There was still no sign of Reynolds or his fishing boat. Lyon, who remained steadfastly committed to his single-minded aim to fight back, decided that if *Krait* did not arrive soon, there was a chance that discipline could start to break down, due to the unease and boredom caused by the constant delay. Determined that this must not be allowed to happen, he now put pressure on Campbell and Davidson to ensure the operatives remained at their peak.

Chapter Seven

Jaywick Begins

In a moment of unusual frustration, Lyon shouted at Davidson and Campbell, 'She has only got bloody 40 miles to come from Sydney. Where the hell is she?' *Krait* had once again struck engine problems and, on the morning of 17 January, the rest of the men in Camp X were starting to feel their leader's frustration. Talking quietly over a steaming cup of tea after a vigorous early morning fitness beasting delivered by Davidson, they suddenly heard a deep chugging from beyond Challenger Head. The noise as yet could not be attributed to anything. Then, to yelps of relief, a small, almost decrepit looking vessel, only slightly longer than a cricket pitch, came into view through the early morning haze. Guns were grabbed and rounds erupted into the morning sky, breaking the tension. As the sailors descended rapidly down the cliff face to meet *Krait*, they were in danger of doing themselves serious damage before they even faced the enemy. Reaching the beach first, Marsh and another member of the team, Leslie 'Tiny' Hage, so named as he was 1.87 metres tall, commandeered HMAS *Lyon* and paddled out to meet *Krait* and Bill Reynolds, who was dropping anchor in the bay.

Bill Reynolds at the wheel of MV *Krait*

As the morning wore on, a sense of reality set in as the crew went about loading the remainder of equipment and provisions that were needed to take them far behind enemy lines. The bulk of the food stores, issued by the Royal Edward Victualling Yard in Sydney on 7 and 8 January, were already on board. They were certainly not going to go hungry. The three-page order, written out in duplicate and signed by the Victualling Stores Officer, covered more than 50 separate items, canned vegetables, meat, fish and fruit; dried fruits; general cooking needs; dry goods such as rice, oatmeal flour, sugar, tea, coffee and cocoa; condensed milk; Vegemite and eight different varieties of jam; condiments, including 24 bottles of chutney and 12 bottles of tomato sauce; biscuits, cheese and chocolate. Liquid beverages included four gallons of lime juice to help ward off scurvy, 12 bottles of whisky (Lyon's preferred tipple), six of brandy and, following a 200-year-old naval tradition, two gallons of rum. These stores would be topped up again in Brisbane and finally in Western Australia, before they left on the actual mission.

What the crew still did not know was their destination, and that *Krait's* exterior had been purposely roughened. The small boat on which Reynolds had rescued so many people actually looked in worse shape than when Lyon and Morris had seen her just over a year ago. While *Krait* was getting ready to be loaded onto *Shillong* for the 12,000-kilometre voyage to Australia, the dockworkers in Bombay had given her a coat of paint and generally spruced her up. On arrival in Fremantle, Commander Long's right-hand man, Denis Emerson-Elliott, a member of SOE Australia and a long-time friend of Lyon and Reynolds, had taken one look and pronounced her unfit for purpose. The vessel no longer looked like an old Japanese fishing boat and would stand out like a sore thumb. However, during the voyage to Sydney from Fremantle, a thorough going over with course sandpaper had made her paintwork appear more authentically dishevelled and distressed.

The ship's down-at-heel appearance did not inspire confidence in the crew, who had no idea that the shabbiness was the means by which they could venture deeply behind enemy lines. It was Davidson's first sight of *Krait* and, knowing their destination was Singapore, he was having a very critical look at this less-than-convincing vessel. Essentially, as Lyon's number two, he could not reveal any lack of confidence in *Krait* for fear that his feelings would be contagious.

Not everyone at Camp X was joining *Krait*. Campbell, having completed his responsibilities in planning and ensuring Jaywick was underway, was remaining behind to oversee the decommissioning of the camp site, with the aid of two recruits, who had not made the final cut. Having taken one look at *Krait*, they weren't sure if they should feel grateful or sad. One of the last to board was Morris with his beloved cat Cleopatra, who was certainly not going to be left behind.

As the equipment and armaments were being loaded, the crew could not help but notice that *Krait* had sunk even lower into the water. However, Bill Reynolds fully understood her capabilities – after all he had sailed the little ship across the Indian Ocean virtually singled-handed. His reassuring manner and often scalding comments if kit wasn't being stowed correctly, kept the crew in check and from not spending too much time wondering just how seaworthy *Krait* was and where they may be heading.

As they prepared to move out into the Hawkesbury, Davidson noticed that the 17-year-old engine, which was idling, was making some very strange noises. Not understanding that *Krait* had worked day after day ferrying survivors from Singapore across to Sumatra and eventually sailed all the way to Ceylon, he mentioned this to Reynolds. He wished he hadn't. The skipper took it as a personal insult, saying, 'Nothing bloody wrong with her!'

With everything stowed, the revs of the engine increased, Reynolds gave the order to weigh anchor. Sailing steadily across Broken Bay, and feeling that a patriotic song was in order, Morris broke into a stirring rendition of 'The British Grenadiers'.

On reaching the open sea, *Krait* turned north and Morris set about settling in his feline friend, who was now officially appointed the ship's mascot. He noted that down below *Krait* was the same grubby little craft he had visited just a year ago. Topside, crew members started working out where they would sleep, hang their hammocks and eat the many meals that the ship's cook Hobbs would prepare in incredibly confined quarters. They were all horrified when Reynolds showed them the toilet facilities, which entailed sitting out over the stern with a bucket on a rope for any necessary ablutions. Loaded to the gunnels *Krait* continued to lumber north in a significant southerly swell, yawing badly, with Hobbs trying to work out how the cooker worked while trying to fix breakfast.

With the extra fuel tanks that had been installed in the refit and the oil drums stored on deck, *Krait* now had the range of an incredible 8,000 nautical miles. Campbell had done a good job provisioning her, with sufficient stores and rations to last the crew for six months. However, as *Krait* sailed on, Reynolds experienced problems with the fuel lines, followed by an acrid smell coming from the engine room, which Lyon immediately recognised as a burning clutch, due to slippage. Some five hours after departure, when the vessel began to lose headway off the coast of Newcastle,

Sharples sent a message requesting a tow. Reynolds hoisted the sail, but in such a swell *Krait* was unable to make it to harbour unaided. The German Deutz Diesel engine was showing her age.

They were eventually taken in tow by the minesweeper HMAS *Peterson*, whose captain was perplexed as to why such a shocking looking vessel was at sea at all, and with an Australian Navy and British army crew. Securing a towline in such a swell was no easy matter. Members of the crew scrambled around on deck, trying to grab the line, only to see it repeatedly disappear over the side. Eventually, it was tied to the king post on the bow, but that was riddled with dry rot and collapsed. To make matters worse, in the attempt to rescue *Krait, Peterson* collided with the smaller vessel, damaging her hull.

Nothing seemed to be going right for the old sea dog Reynolds and, just two miles from harbour, his profanity was at its height. The swearing coming from the engine room only ceased when the engine spluttered into life, allowing *Krait*, in the end, make a fairly dignified entry into harbour, where she would once again have to undertake some significant repairs.

Whilst mooring, Reynolds grabbed a rope to secure the vessel and leapt onto the quayside, only to have the rope snag and unceremoniously dunk him into the water. Surfacing, he was minus his only pair of spectacles. Morris, who was never known to swear, heard words he had never heard before. Lyon and Davidson, who were showing steadfast leadership and kept calm, were privately concerned that such a bad start would have an adverse effect on the crew.

On 20 January, with the clutch repaired and fuel lines thoroughly cleaned, *Krait* made her way out to the open sea, cautiously sailing north, as intelligence reports had been received that Japanese submarines had been sighted further up the coast.

Lyon was not on board, as he had departed for Sydney to meet with Campbell and Reid in the flat in Potts Point. Lyon had a fair idea that the aged Deutz engine on *Krait* was not up to the task and would not last much longer, so he set Campbell the task of trying to find a replacement through the Department of Naval Intelligence.

As *Krait* made the slow progress north, Lyon caught up with the ship, travelling by train.

Krait struggled through turbulent seas and Morris, the only soldier on board besides Lyon, was amused to discover that sea sickness was taking its toll on the sailors, apart from Davidson and Reynolds. The Deutz engine continued to cough and splutter, suffering from multiple ailments. As they approached Coffs Harbour, approximately halfway between Sydney and Brisbane, Reynolds spoke to Lyon and recommended they put into port. 'I don't personally think that the engine will last another hour,' he admitted. This time they made a more dignified entry to the harbour and with great haste set about procuring some first-class engineers. After another engine overhaul and some head scratching and blaspheming, they agreed that the vessel could be put to sea, although both the engineers and Reynolds knew that all they had done was apply some sticking plaster when, in reality, what was needed was major surgery.

They eventually made it to Brisbane, where once again major work on *Krait*'s engine was undertaken. Many parts were worn or not functioning, but no spare parts were available so all replacements had to be re-engineered from scratch, but at least Reynolds was happy that naval engineers were casting a critical eye over his engine. However, with the Deutz proving to be unreliable, Leading Stoker James 'Paddy' McDowell joined the team. Apart from being an expert engineer, he was an experienced merchant seaman, a heavy smoker and a tough Irishman. Shortly afterwards they were joined by another old sea dog, Leading Seaman Kevin 'Cobber' Cain, who had travelled the world in the merchant navy and boasted he had saltwater in his veins. A very experienced seaman, with a placid nature and a well-developed sense of order, he was an excellent addition to the crew.

It was soon determined that the work on the engine would take at least a month. As news filtered back to Sydney of yet another breakdown, Campbell decided to travel north to meet with Lyon. Realising the impact the lack of progress was having on morale, Lyon and Davidson made a very wise decision to send the crew to

Surfers Paradise, to the south of Brisbane, where they could work on their tans and at the same time keep fit and let off some steam. Meanwhile, Lyon set about sourcing material for sarongs – the native wear of Asian fishermen. He discovered that Bert Overell's family owned a large drapery emporium in the city and was delighted to find it stocked patterns very similar to those he had seen fishermen in Indonesia wearing. The Overell family was more than happy to do its bit for the war effort and set about making the simple garments. Lyon, of course, could not divulge where they were heading, or what they were doing, so the Overells were rather puzzled when asked to give the finished sarongs several washes to make them look used and old. Lyon chuckled at the thought of telling the crew members they must wear them, and that all uniforms were to be taken off *Krait* before they left Australia, leaving them with only well-worn, scruffy shorts, lest an unexpected sighting by an enemy plane or surface vessel give them away.

Lyon also busied himself cultivating potential intelligence sources among American servicemen, some of whom were billeted in the homely Anne Hathaway Hotel, where he was staying. Lyon was astonished to find the owner, a lovely middle-aged lady, inflicted a rule of strict temperance under her roof. The typically informal Americans referred to her as 'Mum', and often helped her with the cooking and taught her their home-cooked recipes. Escaping at night to local bars with the Americans, Lyon was to learn much about Japanese activity in the South Pacific. He was a very good listener.

In late February, with their batteries recharged, the sailors returned from their sojourn by the beach and were keen to get underway. With morale now restored to the same level as when they embarked at Refuge Bay, and with additional last minute stores taken on board, including a fair quantity of jam and biscuits, plus fresh bread and eggs, they sailed from Brisbane on 2 March. They had not gone far and were just to the north of Moreton Island when they ran into quite severe weather. Morris recorded that 'we were sailing in what Lyon calmly explained was a force eight gale.

The waves were between 6 and 8 metres. *Krait* was rolling from side to side and her bow was disappearing under the waves with a cracking thud as it rode over each wave's peak.' The most sea Morris had seen back in Wales was when he had cycled to Barry Island one weekend to go for a paddle. Whilst he didn't want to show it, he and other members of the crew were terrified.

Morris was relieved when Davidson calmly said the ship was just behaving like a drunken submarine. As the crew held on tightly, they were horrified to see supplies that had been lashed on deck washed over the side, such was the force of water. Cleopatra, the ship's mascot, was frozen in fright against the bulkhead. As a wave crashed over the stern, the pet Morris had come to love was gone forever.

The loss of Cleo was regarded as a very bad omen by superstitious members of the crew. This was a challenging time for the officers, who had to convince them that *Krait* was not an ill-fated vessel and that she could still get them through to wherever it was they were going. However, their run of bad luck had not yet finished. The storm had scarcely abated when the engine spluttered and coughed, covering the engine room in oil from a fractured pipe. Once again, used spare parts had to be sought while they moored at Tin Can Bay, at the southern end of Fraser Island. Paddy McDowell proved himself to be very resourceful and recruited three engineers from a local shipyard. They too wondered what a beaten up fishing boat was doing in Tin Can Bay with a military and naval crew on board. *Better not to ask,* they thought.

While *Krait* was being repaired, Lyon sent Davidson, who had been experiencing severe shakes and chills from an attack of malaria, to the local hospital for treatment. With so many things going wrong, the crew was amazed by Lyon's indefatigable spirit. Many other men would have cracked up, or given up. There was one member of crew who was not surprised, though – Morris. He had been with Lyon through some very tough and tense times, and had no doubt of the man's calibre and single mindedness. A day or so later, with the engine once more patched up and Davidson back on board, they set sail, watched from the quayside by the civilian engineers. They were speculating where the strange looking vessel was heading, when one said jokingly, 'They're off to sink the bloody Japanese Navy.'

They were anchored just south of Whitsunday Island, to the north of Mackay, when Paddy McDowell, always an early riser, decided to warm up the engine. Morris was his usual self, gently humming a tune as he went about his tasks so as not to disturb those lucky enough to be languishing in their hammocks, when he was rocked by an explosion that severely shook the vessel. Everyone was awake now and all thought they were under attack. While people were trying to figure out what had happened, Morris raced aft, from where the noise originated, peered down into the engine room and saw that a piston had sheared through the engine casing. Reynolds was incandescent with rage and headed below. Everyone kept well away, even Lyon, as Reynolds lost no time in venting his anger on McDowell and sailor Don Russell, his volunteer off-sider. McDowell sensibly acquiesced, but Russell was having none of it. However, it was a mistake to respond to Reynolds' tirade and to underestimate his physical prowess. Although the skipper was the oldest member of the crew, he floored the younger man with a solid punch.

The crew quickly worked out that *Krait* would be going no further. Reynolds was devastated. He had been through many tough times with *Krait* and she had never let him down. While he would later come to terms with accepting that no one was to blame for the engine's fate, he knew that he could be facing a charge of assault for striking a seaman. He also understood that they had been putting off the inevitable. Withdrawing from the engine room, he said calmly to Lyon and the crew, 'She's going to need a new engine.'

Krait was towed to Townsville, where all the equipment was taken off the vessel and the operation officially stood down. Stripped of everything, and with nothing to act as ballast, the ship was then towed with some difficulty to Cairns where, in order to maintain operational readiness and fitness, the crew was sent to Z

Experimental Station. This establishment, in a rambling historic house outside the town, had started out as a wireless relay station for the Allied Intelligence Bureau (AIB) to maintain radio contact with coastwatchers in the islands to Australia's north. However, it was now also serving as a training centre for various operatives working under AIB's umbrella.

As Cairns had been almost completely evacuated due to the perceived threat of a Japanese invasion, the House on the Hill, as it was known, was an ideal location for training of covert activities. While the men were busy keeping fit, Davidson arranged for a transfer to HMAS *Assault*, near Newcastle, followed by a month at sea. He would return to *Assault* in June, to conduct unarmed combat courses with the help of Jaywick's operatives.

Reynolds, however, was no longer part of the operation. Although striking a seaman was a serious offence, in both military and naval terms, he was not formally sanctioned as it was impossible to do so. Although a member of SOE, the reason why he was on the mission, he had refused the offer of a naval commission, so his status was that of a civilian. While the case did not proceed as one of common assault, with Jaywick pretty much dead in the water, *Krait* without an engine and the attack crew marking time, Reynolds decided it was time for him to move on.

Determined one way or another to get back into the war, instead of returning permanently to civilian life, he offered his services to American Intelligence, which was impressed with his credentials, experience and knowledge of the south Pacific and Far East. Joining what was the American equivalent of SOE, Reynolds would eventually be dropped off by a US submarine, behind enemy lines on an island off the south-east tip of Borneo, to gather intelligence. The parting of Reynolds, Lyon, and *Krait* was a bittersweet moment.

A high level meeting, held in Melbourne on 27 March, had decreed that, unless another engine could be found, Jaywick would be postponed indefinitely, sparking a frantic search using every intelligence source available, without result. However, with the mission very much on the back burner, even if an engine were found, the higher levels of authority would take some convincing to get Jaywick back on track.

In the months that had passed since Jaywick was conceived and SOE Australia formed, there had been a number of changes. In February SOE Australia ceased to exist and its chief, Colonel Mott, was relieved of his post and sent back to England. All missions that were in the pipeline were now suspended. Mott was replaced by Colonel Oldham, formerly his 2IC, but it was not until April that General Blamey sanctioned the establishment of Special Operations Australia, or SOA. Although directly answerable to him, the new organisation was similar in its aims to its predecessor and was still under the control of General MacArthur. Jaywick however, remained a purely RAN-SOE mission, funded by SOE in the UK and supported by the Royal Australian Navy, giving it unique status.

In order to gain more strategic support and attention for Jaywick from the upper echelons, Colonel Oldham initiated a typically unorthodox tactic. In order to prove that a small band of determined men, using folboats, could penetrate enemy defences, mine ships at anchor and get away, scott free, he ordered a dummy raid to be carried out on Allied shipping in Townsville. The attack was led on 13 April by a tough, single-minded Australian, Captain Sam Carey, who had been training with a team to limpet mine enemy shipping in Rabaul Harbour. However, the necessary submarine transport was not available, and the mission, code-named Scorpion, had been cancelled.

After arriving by train from Z Experiment Station in Cairns, Carey's highly trained Scorpion men penetrated the defences of Townsville Harbour in their folboats, attached 45 dummy limpet mines to 15 ships and decamped, undetected by those on board and harbour security, on what was a moonlit night. When the tide dropped and the mines were discovered the next morning, sirens sounded and blackouts were ordered, creating panic locally. Although a dummy raid, the realisation that Australia was vulnerable to such an attack was not lost on military and security chiefs. The Townsville raid, whilst being harmless, proved that an attack, such as Lyon planned, was indeed viable.

One morning in June, Lyon received the first news of the fate of *Nankin*, the ship Gabrielle and Clive were on and which had disappeared in the Indian Ocean more than a year previously. Allied intelligence sources had just discovered that the vessel was in Yokohama, Japan, intact, and that all passengers were presumed to be imprisoned somewhere in a Japanese camp. Lyon was overwhelmed with relief, but had also seen with his own eyes the barbarity of which the Japanese were capable. He now had to push from his mind the thoughts of his young wife nursing a baby behind barbed wire.

Gabrielle and Clive had been in their cabin on board *Nankin* when they and other passengers were woken on the morning of 10 May 1942, at about 0800 hours, to the sound of an aircraft overhead. This gave them cause for anxiety, as they were in mid-ocean, far from land, and at first it was hoped that the plane was British or American, but by mid-morning a rumour spread that it may have been a spotter for an enemy surface raider. Shortly afterwards, when the aircraft flew over the ship at a much lower altitude, attempting to wipe out the vessel's radio mast, an officer confirmed that it must be from a surface raider. The crew moved rapidly to man deck-mounted machine guns, at the same time scouring the surrounding sea for any sign of a submarine.

Although the plane strafed *Nankin*, fire from the ship's machine guns managed to prevent it from damaging the radio aerial. Clutching Clive, Gabrielle turned her back on the sound of gunfire, touching for luck the diamond brooch on her lapel that her husband had given to her, fashioned in the shape of three bears. A vessel soon came into view and the thud of its deck gun could be heard, as it attempted to secure its range on its target. *Nankin*'s small foredeck gun went into action, but it lacked the firepower of the raider's armament. Keeping well out of range, the enemy ship proceeded to straddle *Nankin* with shells from side to side, fore and aft, until it got the exact range. *Nankin*'s Captain Stratford ordered the ship's operator to send out an SOS.

Now that the raider had established *Nankin*'s exact range there was a tremendous and sickening crash as the ship was holed, just above the waterline on the port bow. Stratford decided that, with women and children aboard, he had no alternative but to abandon ship, a sensible decision given that, unbeknown to the passengers, *Nankin* was loaded with a considerable amount of high explosives.

In an orderly evacuation and with little panic, Gabrielle and Clive made it safely into a lifeboat at around 1430 hours. Incredibly, of just over 340 passengers and crew, only two crew members had been killed. Convinced that the attacker was Japanese, the rest of the crew, along with the passengers, waited helplessly in the lifeboats as the predatory vessel continued to bear down on them, and screamed as the aircraft flew low overhead, expecting to be machine-gunned. It was with a great sense of relief that they noticed a German flag had been raised off the raider's stern. The vessel was the 6,000-ton *Thor*.

Before finally abandoning his vessel Captain Stratford, who remained calm and collected throughout the ordeal, ordered the engines to be put out of action and the sea cocks opened, in order to scuttle the ship. Anticipating this, the Germans rapidly put on board a prize crew, which managed to stem the flow of water and save the ship. After a few days, they had repaired the engines to enable *Nankin* to proceed under her own power.

When the passengers were taken aboard the raider, its crew were surprised by the large number of women and children. Gabrielle, Clive, and the other passengers were all accommodated on the lower deck of the ship, well below the waterline. It was very cramped and, once underway, the forced air ventilation did not appear to be functioning, making conditions uncomfortably hot and stuffy. However, the food and treatment were reasonably good and everyone was allowed on deck, morning and afternoon, for a period of one hour.

Their stay on *Thor* was temporary and they were transferred to two other German vessels, *Regensburg* and *Dresden,* which took them to Yokohama. The captives were naturally apprehensive, but their captors treated them well for the duration of the voyage. During World War I, *Regensburg*'s captain had been a prisoner of war on the Isle of Wight, while *Dresden*'s skipper had been interned in Australia, and it was thought this was the reason for the good treatment.

From Yokohama, Gabrielle and Clive were eventually transferred to Fukushima Internment Camp Number 12, where they would spend the rest of the war. It was from here, in April 1944, almost two years after their disappearance, that news they were definitely alive and well would reach Lyon, via the International Red Cross, putting an end to his private suffering.

Back in Brisbane, shortly after receiving the news about his wife and child, in mid-June Lyon and Davidson met (not for the first time) the journalist Lorraine Stumm, on this occasion accompanied by her sister Margot. That evening they dined at Lennon's Hotel, which essentially was the heart of American intelligence and power in the region. Stumm, who was well connected, was aware that Davidson and Lyon were training commandoes at a secret camp in Cairns for an operation behind enemy lines. Over dinner, she fully grasped and was able to understand Ivan Lyon's deep desire and motivation to do some real damage to Japanese interests.

Enjoying a very enjoyable respite over fillet steak and a fine bottle of Veuve Clicquot, Lyon explained to Lorraine and Margot how his wife and one-year-old son were believed to have been captured by an enemy ship and were now in Japan. Addressing his three fellow diners Lyon said, 'I gave Gabrielle a little diamond brooch in the shape of three bears. You'll see, she will come out of prison camp wearing it. I'm sure they won't get it from her.'

There was more good news. Lyon had been promoted to major, and both he and Morris had been officially recognised for their work in evacuating those lucky enough to flee Singapore, onto the escape route through Sumatra. Morris had been awarded a British Empire Medal, while Lyon had been made a Member of the British Empire, the honour also received by Reynolds for his rescue work. Morris was justifiably proud of his BEM and his letter of appointment from King George VI.

In even more good news, a new engine to replace the old Deutz had been located by Emerson-Elliott in Hobart, Tasmania – a brand new 6L 103 horsepower Gardner Diesel, capable of propelling the 60-ton boat at an estimated top speed of 12 knots. Although the engine had been earmarked for the army, Emerson-Elliott's immediate boss, Director of Naval Intelligence Commander Long, made sure that the RAN and SOE had first claim, and arranged for it to be shipped to Cairns.

A number of modifications needed to be made to the vessel before the engine was fitted, which then had to go through a period of being run in. All in all, the work took two months to complete. *Krait* still had a shambolic appearance, but her heartbeat was now much stronger and steadier. The ship was also much tougher and heavier, the deck having been 'bullet proofed' with a thick layer of bituminous material. Davidson felt the additional weight would adversely affect her handling – something he only shared with Lyon.

Apart from the addition of McDowell and Cain to the team in Brisbane, there had been a number of other crew changes while the ship was in Cairns. Hobbs the cook, who was rather temperamental and had wanted to quit while at Camp X, only to be coerced into staying by Jock Campbell, had finally left. His replacement was a cheery, curly-haired army corporal, Andrew Crilly, who was on the lookout for some adventure. When he had heard that a cook was needed for hazardous service he applied, even though his culinary skills were limited to boiling water, opening up cans of food and making pancakes, a talent that earned him the title 'Pancake Andy'. As the only 'cooking' necessary was to heat up the contents of canned food and boil rehydrated dried vegetables and mutton, his ability to rustle up pancakes was a bonus.

Two of the final eight who had made the cut at Camp X had also left, along with Bert Overell and the third sailor, 'Tiny' Hage, as the plan to attack shore installations had now been scrapped. Gort Chester, who was to have been in charge of *Krait* while the raiding party was away, had been recalled to lead another operation behind the lines in British North Borneo. Lyon was saddened by the departure of Chester, an extremely able officer and leader.

With both Overell and Chester gone, Lyon needed another officer for the raiding party. He selected Robert Page, a fresh-faced Australian army lieutenant, who had put his medical training at Sydney University on hold in order to enlist. As a member of Carey's party, which had carried out the dummy raid in Townsville, Page was experienced in handling limpets. His additional medical knowledge was certainly welcomed by Taffy Morris.

The final two members to join the team, just three weeks before *Krait* sailed, were a telegraphist and navigator. The original telegraphist, Don Sharples, who was not keen to remain with the mission, had gone with the rest of the team to HMAS *Assault* to assist Davidson demonstrate unarmed combat. While there he had mentioned his dissatisfaction to another telegraphist, Horrie Young. Fed up with Newcastle's cold winter weather and lured by a substantial cash bonus, generally referred to as 'danger money', he arranged to swap with Sharples and travelled north to warmer climes.

With Reynolds now gone, Lyon had the very difficult task of recruiting a navigator with intimate knowledge of Australian waters and the route *Krait* was to take from Western Australia to Singapore. Long suggested an old shipmate from his training days, Lieutenant Edward Carse, a reservist and an experienced sailor and navigator, who was training Asian sailors at Z Experimental Station. As Lyon needed a navigator with knowledge of local tides and currents, Carse got the job.

The final 14 chosen for the mission were operatives Lyon, Davidson, Page, Huston, Falls and Jones; reservists Berryman and Marsh; navigator Carse, engineer McDowell, medic Morris, seaman Cain, telegraphist Young and finally Crilly the cook, who turned out to be one of the most important members of the crew. He was a fast learner and was soon converting dehydrated and canned rations into palatable meals. He and Morris, being both regular army in a predominantly naval crew, quickly bonded to create a strong friendship, and Morris often offered Crilly kind words of support in what he saw to be a thankless task of feeding the crew three times a day. Nevertheless, all were very pleased to have such a willing chef, even though the ingredients at his disposal were extremely limited.

Carse fired up the new engine early in the morning of 8 August and set a course for Cape York Peninsula, the northernmost tip of Australia. The new navigator had grave concerns over the ship's seaworthiness, given her payload and the waters through which *Krait* was to sail. However, morale was high among the rest of the crew, as they set out on an adventure of a lifetime. Even at this stage, no one but the four officers knew the final destination.

As they continued on their passage northwest, the recently applied armour plating on the deck continued to make the boat wallow and kept her low in the water. They were also weighed down by fuel, supplies for four months, ammunition, 45 limpet mines, two Lewis guns, two Bren guns, eight Sten guns, and eight Owen guns. Added to this, was a substantial quantity of Dutch Guilders, 70 kilograms of carefully stowed plastic explosive and 200 hand grenades. In Carse's opinion, *Krait* was a floating time bomb.

The voyage took them around the north of Australia, past Thursday Island where Lyon received final secret instructions sent by Commander Long, and on through the Torres Strait. Apart from a temporary grounding on one of the reefs, which caused no damage, the voyage was incident free. It was a scenic route and the crew was so busy marvelling at the coral and wildlife on the reefs that the officers had to remind them to keep a constant lookout for enemy spotter planes. However, their concentration was occasionally unavoidably broken by schools of friendly dolphins riding in *Krait*'s wake and on one memorable occasion by a large whale, which breached and came crashing down with a thunderous impact that reverberated right through the vessel, before coming alongside as if it wanted to keep the same pace and course. Without warning, it was attacked by sharks, which thrashed their tail fins as they sought to take chunks out of the much larger creature, until it took refuge by diving into the deep, and disappeared from sight.

After rounding Cape York, *Krait* began crossing the Gulf of Carpentaria on the morning of 17 August. Lyon and Davidson had instilled maximum vigilance into the crew, although most felt that, as they were skirting the coast of Australia, they were safe. However, as there had been reports of Japanese activity and hostile attacks, Morris was standing on a 50-gallon oil drum with his head poked through a hatch in the rear awning, looking towards the bow and keeping watch for enemy spotter planes and patrol vessels. They were in fact as close, and if not closer, to Japanese attack than they would be throughout their voyage. Nearby Horn Island, which housed thousands of Allied troops, was constantly being bombed by the Japanese. However, the atmosphere on board was good, and everyone wished Ivan Lyon a happy 28th birthday.

Morris had the sun on his face and wind in his hair as he scanned the horizon from his oil drum. Below him, most of the crew sat in a circle cleaning and checking weapons – a routine chore after breakfast. The mess area into which Morris's legs were protruding was littered with plates and condiments waiting to be cleared. Cain, out of sight of Morris, was trying to free a round of ammunition jammed in the circular magazine of a Lewis gun that he was cleaning, when the weapon accidentally discharged. Believing they were under attack, people dived for cover as the round whistled across the messing area, smashing a tomato sauce bottle before embedding itself in the hull. Everyone took stock to see who was injured, as a thick blood-like substance was splattered everywhere. Page promptly sprang into action and quickly established that what he at first thought was blood, splattered across the roof and engine room cover, was actually tomato sauce.

There were, however, two casualties, one serious. Morris, who had experienced an ice-like penetration in his ankle, fainted and fell down through the hatch and onto the deck. It was never established if it were the live round or a piece of glass from the bottle but, whatever the projectile was, it had torn through an artery in Morris's lower leg. He was now losing blood at a dangerous rate and falling into a state of shock. While a couple of crew members held the injured leg aloft to help reduce the blood flow, Page poked about trying to find the ends of the artery, while a third assistant forced brandy into Morris's mouth, which he instinctively gulped. Realising this was not going to be a short operation, Page applied a tourniquet to the upper leg before he began the difficult and delicate task of stitching Morris's arteries back together again, using an oversized, rather blunt needle and cat gut, before smothering the wound with sulphanilamide powder. Considering he was not a qualified doctor, Page did a fantastic job and undoubtedly saved Morris's life. The whole operation took two hours and thankfully, the bottle of brandy from the ship's stores had the required analgesic effect.

The second casualty was Berryman who, like Morris, had been peppered with shards of glass. Both were confined to their hammocks, and it took Page many painstaking hours to remove the remaining glass fragments from both men. Morris's injury would take weeks to heal and, although Lyon asked if he wanted to receive further medical attention on shore, he declined the offer, fearful of not proceeding on the mission and letting Lyon and his teammates down. Later that evening, Morris was heard to be gently singing as he swung to and fro in his hammock.

Lyon had discussed with Carse the issue of how *Krait* had been handling. Since the application of the thick bulletproof coating to the deck, the vessel was top heavy, especially in swells and rough seas. Her freeboard had also been reduced significantly, causing the deck to become constantly awash. Taking advantage of the tranquil waters and fine weather, Lyon ordered the crew to lever the thick bulletproof layer from the deck and heave it over the side, reducing the weight by an estimated two tons. Now rid of her burden, and with her bow riding high in the water, the ship was able to increase speed.

As *Krait* cruised past Cape Wessel, off the Northern Territory, Carse and Lyon acknowledged that the charts supplied for this section of the coast were extremely inaccurate. Some reefs and islands were unmarked and only by keeping a vigilant lookout had they kept out of danger. On an early morning watch, just as dawn was breaking, Jones suddenly shouted, 'Sandbar, dead ahead,

50 yards!' Lyon, who was at the wheel, spun it to the right, causing *Krait* to lurch to starboard, and pulled back the throttle to stop engines. Soon after there were two gentle thuds as the keel hit a sandbank.

Lyon estimated they were afloat in two fathoms of water. Engaging the engine at low revs, he edged the vessel forward and, when the light increased, they saw that they were surrounded by sandbars and coral. Checking the inaccurate charts, Lyon estimated they were inside a circular reef off Adele Island. He checked the pilot's book and noted that the entrance was to the north-east. They had accidentally entered the inner reef in the dark and, if they got in, they must be able to get out. The crew was becoming tense, but Davidson and Lyon were extremely calm as they plotted their exit from a potentially perilous situation. The pilot book noted that no attempt should be made to enter Adele Reef without excellent local knowledge, the one narrow entrance was noted to be 'very foul'. Gently easing forward, in thankfully calm seas, *Krait* edged her way out of the reef into the open sea. Once they were in clear water, Lyon thrust the throttle forward and, breathing a sigh of relief, headed towards the coast of Western Australia.

Their final port of call, before leaving Australia, was Exmouth Gulf or, more precisely, the US Naval Base, known as Operation Potshot. The voyage was trouble free, apart from encountering very heavy seas near the Monte Bello Islands, which sent *Krait* pitching forward, her bow descending under the waves. However, even though the boat was taking on significant amounts of water, Lyon remained absolutely calm, which was highly reassuring to the less experienced crew members.

Finally, after 18 days at sea, *Krait* arrived at Exmouth Gulf on 26 August, where the Americans had established their large base, servicing a submarine fleet tasked to hunting down Japanese vessels. *Krait*'s crew was quickly befriended by the Americans on board USS *Chanticleer*, a submarine repair vessel that was berthed alongside. *Chanticleer*'s skipper, Captain Hawes, arranged for half of *Krait*'s crew to be assigned quarters ashore, which gave those remaining on board much more room.

Admiral Christie, the Commander of the base, knew where *Krait* was headed, and issued instructions to fulfill all requests for assistance. He and Hawes hosted the entire Jaywick team to dinner in the mess. Not believing they had sailed the scruffy looking fishing boat from Cairns, Hawes challenged Carse, saying, 'Don't expect an old sailor like me to swallow a yarn that you have sailed around Australia in that scow. Why, I wouldn't take that thing to sea for a Texas oil well.' Although Christie knew the truth and *Krait*'s final destination, he remained tight-lipped.

No one on board Krait had enjoyed American hospitality before, and revelled in the experience. However, in between bouts of eating copious amounts of rich ice cream, the crew trained hard and practised set drills. One involved a plan of action, should they be intercepted.

The ship had a small, flat-bottomed dinghy into which Davidson had inserted two copper tubes. Attached to these were four-metre lengths of rubber tubing, onto which gas masks were fitted to serve as improvised diving masks. If intercepted, Lyon and Jones, who were small boned and deeply tanned and could pass as natives at a pinch, would enter the dinghy with empty water cans and paddle across to the intercepting vessel. Unbeknown to the enemy, concealed in the water below the dinghy were two operatives, breathing through the improvised masks. As the dinghy came alongside the enemy vessel, they would place two short-fused limpet mines on the hull below the waterline. They would then swim underwater to the other side of the vessel, away from the mines, which were set to detonate in two minutes. Meanwhile, hidden behind *Krait*'s awning, the remainder of the crew, armed to the teeth with Lewis, Owen, and Sten guns, would prepare to open fire if detected. They practised this drill repeatedly, carefully guided and critiqued by Davidson, becoming so adept at the approach and manoeuvre that they felt, if challenged, they had a damn good chance of coming out on top.

Davidson also took receipt of various items, amounting to a payload of more than 380 kilograms, which had been flown from Melbourne, ranging from explosives to various protective and navigational equipment, binoculars, a long-range telescope, anti-glare glasses, spare parts for *Krait* and parcels and mail for the crew. However, he was extremely displeased with the new folboats that had also been dispatched, made on his instructions and the exact specifications for which had been spelled out. There was no option but to instruct the crew to make the necessary modifications, while he drafted a very tersely-worded report expressing his fury and absolute dismay at being supplied with substandard equipment for such a dangerous mission.

Much still needed to be done prior to setting out on the mission, readying the ship for its lengthy voyage, and taking on more stores, including clothing, mosquito nets, hurricane lamps, torches, blankets, towels, cutlery and enamel plates. Foodstuffs included additional stocks of most items taken on board in Sydney, along with two cases each of lime and orange juice, another two gallons of rum and 600 gallons of water. Also loaded on board were 1000 gallons of diesel oil, 80 gallons of lubricating oil, 12 gallons of petrol and eight gallons of kerosene.

Krait was also loaded up with fresh food and provisions from the American ship, and engineers gave the sorry looking fishing boat a thorough overhaul. The deck was painted a dull grey colour, to make the vessel more difficult to spot from the air. As inquisitive as the Americans were, asking the crew where they were heading, all they could say was they didn't know. Those who did remained tight-lipped. When asked what the oil drum fixture over the exhaust was – an ingenious silencer that Paddy McDowell had fitted – Morris explained, 'It makes us run more quietly and attracts less attention.' It was only then that some of the engineers suspected this unassuming boat was headed for somewhere extremely dangerous.

That day, Lyon wrote a letter to his family, commenting that after the war he might become a first-class club bore, that he was looking very black and leathery, and that it would take a considerable time after the war for him to become his old self. On a far more personal note, he added that if he had his wife and young son with him, he would be a happy man.

There was no hint in his letter of the impending danger that lay ahead.

Chapter Eight

Into the Lyon's Den

A few hours before Krait was due to set sail from Exmouth Gulf, a telegram arrived at the base, informing Leading Telegraphist Young that his wife had given birth to a boy. This was felt to be a good omen and the news lightened the mood on what was an otherwise somber departure for most of the crew, who knew they were venturing into the unknown.

After slipping alongside SS *Ondina* – a submarine supply tanker – for their last refuelling and fresh water, it was finally time to depart. After saying farewell to their American friends and thanking them for their hospitality, they set sail at 17.30 hours on the evening of 1 September, gently proceeding out of Exmouth Gulf. One minute into their voyage, the intermediate propeller shaft fractured and *Krait*'s bow dipped her nose into the water as she lost forward momentum.

The atmosphere on the boat was one of utter frustration, and the tension could be cut with a knife. Lyon ordered the anchor to be dropped in five fathoms to prevent them drifting aimlessly and ordered Young to radio to seek assistance. *Better that this should happen here*, thought Carse, *than a thousand miles behind enemy lines*. The mood picked up when, an hour and three-quarters later, *Chanticleer* entered the harbour. Taking the dinghy, Lyon immediately rowed over to where the *Chanticleer* was moored, and shortly afterwards a motorboat towed *Krait* alongside to allow the necessary repairs to be undertaken. US engineers removed the drive shaft and brazed it back together, but it could not be refitted until the following day when it was cooled. The engineers stressed that it was a temporary repair and that they should get a proper job done as soon as they could.

At 1400 the next day, as *Krait* fired up her engine and gently eased away from the harbour into the open sea, destination still unknown, the US sailors shouted, 'Get that shaft fixed as soon as you can!', unaware that the little ship was about to embark on a voyage of almost 8,000 kilometres, deep behind enemy lines, in the knowledge that if they were caught, they would all surely die.

Morris wondered how long it would be until they returned to Australia. What lay ahead was anyone's guess. *All they needed was a little bit of luck,* Lyon thought. Davidson had done more than his best, training what was essentially a handpicked company of men. *If failure was going to happen, it would not be because of any lack of preparation or calibre of these fine individuals,* thought Lyon.

Ducking his head into the engine room to speak to Paddy McDowell, Lyon shouted over the roar of the engine, 'Do you think the shaft will hold, Paddy?' To which he calmly replied, 'They have done a great job, sir'.

While Lyon missed Reynolds, he had formed a deep respect for the capabilities of McDowell, who tended his noisy, smelly engine like a baby. Paddy was indeed a round peg in a round hole, and was an excellent mentor to a young crew.

No sooner had they rounded the northern cape of Exmouth Gulf, a tremendous wind struck them, along with an extremely fast-moving rip tide. With the ship beam on to a force seven sea, Lyon immediately ordered the sail to be reefed, as it was destabilising the vessel. The deck was awash with heavy seas battering the port bow. Young, who was comfortably riding out the turbulence in his hammock, was violently ejected as a huge wave struck, sending a shudder throughout the entire vessel and a wall of water across the deck that swept Young from his hammock. Had it not been for Marsh's very quick thinking and agility in grabbing him, he would have been swept overboard into the raging sea.

Meanwhile, Lyon was in the wheelhouse, fighting to bring the bow around to avoid constant bombardment of the port bow. Davidson attempted to come up on deck from below, but was washed back by huge volumes of green water forcing its way through the hatch. The crew heard and felt the bow crashing down into the ocean as the boat listed severely, throwing anyone still standing off their feet.

The crew held its collective breath, waiting for the small ship to fight back and emerge from the torrent. Where many other vessels would have faltered, *Krait* eventually rose from the froth with a shudder, and Lyon – aided by Carse – managed to swing the bow around head on, into the full force of the gale. Morris, wrapped around the rails by the engine room, which had been totally submerged at one point thought that his time had come.

Then, like the flick of a switch, the weather changed dramatically. Carse and Lyon agreed that, had they not disposed of the bulletproof deck, they may well not have survived the surging tidal rip which, accompanied by a southerly gale force wind, had created the perfect storm.

After a good night's rest, the ensuing calm seemed an appropriate moment to brief the crew about the mission and their final destination. Not without some drama, Lyon and Davidson jointly unwrapped the Japanese ensign, or 'the poached egg', as they called it. Displaying the flag aloft with his two hands, Davidson announced, 'It's far too clean, lads. They would wise up to us straight away if we flew this. Let's give it a good kicking.' He then threw it on the deck, where the crew gleefully danced and stamped all over it. It was like watching an act of defiance and intent at striking back. By the time they had finished, along with the application of some engine oil, the flag resembled a dirty rag, a fitting accompaniment for the down-at-heel *Krait*.

Lyon then spoke calmly as he said, 'Many of you will have been thinking of where we may be going. You have all, each and every one of you, been handpicked, and your training has been to condition you for the most serious of endeavours. I know some of you think we are going to attack the Japanese on Java, but I have to tell you that we are going far further. We are going to strike at the beating heart of the new Japanese Asian Empire. Singapore is our destination.' On this announcement, and after the frolicking of the crew in degrading the Japanese ensign, the crew's shock was palpable. Lyon's and Davidson's little piece of theatre had worked well.

Lyon stated that to succeed against the might of the Japanese invaders they would have to be a like a chameleon and blend into the environment. 'Taffy knows,' he said, 'that this boat will provide us with the best possible camouflage. Just as this small vessel was responsible for rescuing many people and delivering them to safety in the waters off Sumatra, we will now be responsible for delivering a vengeful blow at the heart of our enemy.'

Morale is high with the crew of Krait en route to Singapore with Japanese flag flying from the stern

Carse was starting to get edgy as he set *Krait* on a direct course for the Lombok Strait. All knew that this was possibly the first point where they could encounter the Japanese, either because of the proximity of the land, or by being intercepted at sea. However, this eventuality had been covered in the planning stages. Davidson now gave them a lesson on how to correctly fold and put on a native sarong, hopefully allowing them to pass for native fishermen if spotted. To further the disguise, they were to darken their skin using a specially prepared concoction from a famous Australian cosmetics house. Lyon and Davidson, always thinking ahead, had decided to apply it the night before, only to discover that the results were not as expected. The spirit-based substance stung when applied to sensitive regions, so eyes must be avoided as well as private parts, which were covered by the sarongs.

The even colouring they were seeking was far from satisfactory as it formed streaks to those with fair skin, to the great amusement of the crew. However, they still had three members who could be used as deck decoys as they were so deeply tanned they could pass for Asian Orientals.

Lyon thought the disguises might not stand up to close scrutiny, but one thing was for sure, they did look a frightening bunch. Lyon made such a convincing Asian that he joked that his long and ancestral family line must, at some stage, have had a passionate encounter with an indigenous native. Should they spot a potentially hostile aircraft or surface vessel, Davidson explained that Lyon, Jones and Carse would stay on deck. The remainder, taking their weapons, would go to the stern and hide beneath the canvas awning.

Carse, with his deeply-lined dark skin would remain at the wheel as he could easily pass as a Chinese skipper. The final member to remain in plain sight was Jones, who passed the test with flying colours. With his thin, muscular features, narrowing eye cavities, a deep tan and jet black hair, he could actually pass as a Japanese. Clearly, not only temperament, physical and psychological resilience had been taken into account during the selection process.

Following the briefing, Lyon joined Carse in the wheelhouse to check on their progress. Carse observed, 'They look a motley bunch. I hope we get through the Lombok Strait without having to test our contingency plan.'

'Fear not,' said Lyon. 'They will acquit themselves well should the need arise. I know certain danger lies ahead, but this small vessel is a veteran of these waters and remained unchallenged when swarms of Japanese aircraft and ships hunted those escaping from Singapore. I don't want any of the crew to ever be complacent, but I know we have better odds of pulling this off than many give us credit.'

On hearing Lyon's words, Carse had to admit that he felt better. His commander had shared his experience, reassuring him in a calm manner. Nevertheless, Carse nervously scanned the horizon.

Lyon, ever a stickler for security, had issued strict instructions lest the slightest slip-up betray their presence to the enemy. No toilet paper was to be used – a bucket of sea water and a pebble for wiping; food labels had to be removed and destroyed, along with the tins; and smoking was banned, as butts of Western-made cigarettes and matches could tip off collaborators that an enemy vessel was in their waters.

Carse was further calmed when he read the Admiralty pilot book for covering the eastern archipelago, which stated that, during September, weather conditions were humid, hazy, and with low visibility. Crew members were on watch, expecting the volcanic peaks of Mount Agung on Bali and Mount Rinjani, to emerge on the horizon, one to the west and the other to the east. However, they did not come into view as expected as *Krait* was to the west of the Lombok Strait, which, according to the ship's log, can only be put down to straying from the planned course. This deviation put out the timetable and was recorded in *Kraits* log 7 September,

'Owing to making a faulty landfall altered course midnight due South and slowed down to 4 kts'

Carse breathed a huge sigh of relief when he finally spotted 'Nusa Besar' (actually Nusa Penida, or Priest Island in Balinese), which stood like a guard shadowing the western entry to the Lombok Strait. It had been planned to anchor there but the charts showed the water to be far too deep and, in any case, what was thought to be an uninhabited island had a significant amount of activity on it. As *Krait* approached the strait, the crew could feel the strength of the water pushing against the bow of the vessel. Morris observed that it felt like a giant hand, trying to propel them backwards. As they proceeded, with everyone on sharp lookout, they noted a large log floating in the water. The water around it seemed to be thrashing, and as they moved closer they could see a school of sharks aimlessly biting the log. This further added to the tension, as not only was the ferocious tide attacking them, but searchlights could also be seen further to the west where they knew there was a large Japanese airbase at Denpasar on Bali Island.

It was dusk when the two mountainous volcanoes came into view on Bali and Lombok. It was a sight to behold, as most of the crew had never seen anything like it in their lives.

The surge of tide pouring out of the Java Sea, southwards into the Indian Ocean, was too much for poor *Krait,* and at times she was actually moving astern. Carse noted in the log,

'So in spite of a maximum speed, a glorious six-and-a-half knots, we are steadily losing ground.'

For hours, the crew looked tensely at the coast of Bali, the headlamps of enemy vehicles revealing that they were making no headway. In the early hours of the morning they were still fighting the currents in the darkness when Lyon spotted what he thought was a predatory vessel approaching. He was sure it was a three-masted cruiser.

'Steady, lads,' he cautioned, as the vessel closed to what he thought was about one nautical mile. The only sound was that of weapons being cocked under the awning. However, it was a false alarm. Lyon, who was credited with razor vision, had been looking at a large tidal wave, which he thought was a bow wave, and the three masts were actually tall trees on top of a hill.

Having noted that the pilot book advised that haziness was to be expected at this time of the year, they were further dismayed when the next day dawned as clear as a bell. Noticing that a military base to the east on Lombok was shrouded in a light fog, Davidson stood on the port side of the vessel to take photographs of Mount Agung on Bali. However Carse, in an unusual moment of emotional honesty, summed up that night when he wrote, *Thank Christ we are through the strait, this war is certainly hard on the nervous system.*

As they cruised towards the Kangean archipelago, at what seemed to be an excruciatingly slow speed, they sighted many surface vessels until, finally, the haze appeared and descended like a lifesaving curtain to shroud *Krait*'s northward advance. Morale lifted immediately, with Crilly serving a well-earned steaming hot brew of sweet tea and Morris breaking out with a song, 'Scot's Wha Hae', his favourite Robert Burns' ballad, prompting McDowell to accompany him in his first and only duet, while Page and Davidson joined in by whistling. The crew would become wise to the fact that Morris's cheerful choice of song was an indication of the level of danger or relief at having come through a dangerous situation, while songs such as 'The British Grenadiers' or 'Men of Harlech' were a clear signal for vigilance and preparedness.

Not having been spotted or challenged, Carse turned to port, setting a heading north-west towards Borneo and the Karimata Islands. The only concern so far for both Lyon and Davidson was Carse, and how he would stand up under pressure. The navigator was a key member of the crew, on whom the success or failure of the mission hung. Even though *Krait* was now well behind Japanese lines, Lyon had evaluated how individuals reacted for the first time to being in close proximity of the enemy, and he would write this period up in his report stating, 'their complete calm was most encouraging'.

The next period of the voyage was tense but thankfully uneventful, the senior officers became concerned that the crew could start to become complacent due to the lack of a perceived 'clear and present danger'. Under Lyon's instruction, Davidson drilled the crew hard, constantly calling them to battle stations and rehearsing the action they would take if intercepted.

Lyon, Davidson and Carse took turns navigating *Krait* from the wheelhouse, the only place where there was room to spread a chart. Morris and Cain took the helm and stood watch, duties they would have to perform for the 14 days and nights that the folboat crews were away.

On 10 September, eight days into their mission, Carse recorded in the log,

`The morale of the crew is excellent. Our cook Corporal Crilly is doing a marvellous job in making all the meals tasty in spite of bad weather and worse conditions. Everyone was pleased to hear Italy had thrown in the towel, freeing up the Mediterranean fleet. By dark tonight we will be across the main shipping routes from Surabaya and Batavia to Balik Papuan, Timor, and all ports using the Macassar Strait. Our lookouts are particularly keen and so far have sighted any objects long before we could possibly have been seen by them. We have ample supplies of everything except water, which is rationed to three cups of tea a day and a water bottle every three days. Our engineer Leading Stoker McDowell has been invaluable. He has worked day and night, training the crew and operatives to help him in his duties and to operate the engine should anything happen to him, as well as servicing and tending the engine. In fact, he looks after the engine better and treats it more carefully than a mother would a baby. No matter how long the hours, he works away, stopping troubles before they have developed, and always cheerful and happy. No man could be better suited to the job than he is. Lieutenant Page has one main fault. He is always trying to doctor someone up. His latest suggestion is to put all hands on a course of Dr Bland's Pills. For the sake of their health, he puts it, but I think it is to study their reactions while undergoing the said course. The success which has so far attended our efforts may be likely to create over confidence in the crew, but they are so well chosen, and so keen, that I do not think it very likely.`

While morale on board remained incredibly high, given their location and the task they were about to undertake, not everything was good. The beer they had stowed on board had been depleted, and the empties disposed of by smashing them and dropping the glass over the side. However, while the beer had run out, the Navy lads on board and who were of age, received their traditional rum ration and a standard tot was served each evening by Davidson, who screwed the top off a large bottle and tipped the prescribed tots into eagerly awaiting mugs. Morris, who enjoyed a pint of bitter, simply could not develop a taste for what he said was a 'noxious substance' and 'worse than my grandmother's cough medicine'. He tried watering it down and sweetened it with sugar, to no avail. He later regretted that he never thought to add some lime juice from the stores. However, his ration was put aside and, by the time he returned to Exmouth Gulf, his allocation amounted to four two-pint flagons, making him a very popular man and able to barter with US sailors, who were on strictly dry ships.

Everyone was in good health apart from Carse, whose eyesight was not good and was suffering with the glare from the sun. Lyon and Davidson understood that this on its own could account for Carse's edginess. Morris had picked up the only injury so far, but his wounded ankle seemed stubbornly reluctant to heal, although thankfully no infection had set in. As they neared the equator, the deck became too hot to stand on, and the crew rushed to where the freeboard was lowest as it would be awash with seawater. Carse was pleased that *Krait* had settled more into the water, her handling greatly improved since the removal of the bulletproof coating from the deck.

The log noted that the sailing vessels were,

all apparently engaged in coastal trade along the coast of Borneo, as we have seen none since we started to cross the Caramata Strait.'

However, the crew noticed that as soon as native and coastal vessels came into sight, they would invariably alter course. The Japanese flag was being flown in an attempt not to attract Japanese attention, but no one had realised the effect it would have on native vessels, who beat a hasty retreat.

Nevertheless, their mettle was severely tested on 13 September when, nearing Pelapis Island, they were surrounded by a large junk and eight other craft with nondescript rigging. Even though *Krait* looked like a local vessel, no one could guarantee that suspicions would not be aroused. The predesignated members of crew remained in the wheelhouse, while Davidson saw that the crew was at action stations under the awning, armed with weapons, and hand grenades. This encounter, which fortunately came to nothing once the Japanese flag was spotted, nevertheless heightened the need for vigilance and created the necessary edge to sharpen the crew members, although undoubtedly raising adrenaline levels. The next day Carse recorded,

'If we survive the next two days, the operation should be carried out successfully, and then for our return journey. The main topic of conversation these days is of course the job in hand, coupled with the news of Italy's downfall and the German defence of the Vatican City. These factors, together with Russia's remarkable advances, seem to indicate an end to the European war before Christmas, and increased activities in these waters. Fortune so far has been very good to us, and providing she remains kind, we will all be eating dinner in Australia this day next month.'

When Lyon and Reynolds were originally discussing the possibility of striking back at Singapore, Reynolds had highlighted Pompong Island as a potential hideout for *Krait*. It was a place with which he was very familiar, having rescued survivors of HMS *Kuala*, who were stranded there after the ship was bombed. However, as Carse navigated through the Temiang Strait and approached Pompong, they saw that it was now frequented by fishing boats. The senior officers concluded that, since Singapore's invasion, fishermen had moved further afield in fear of coming into contact with the Japanese. This put Pompong out of the question. Lyon also decided that his original choice of hiding place in Sumatra's Kampar River estuary should also be scrapped, as a boat hanging around for that length of time would be conspicuous.

Krait continued around the shoreline of Pompong, steering away from the fishing vessels when, to the horror of the crew on watch, they saw a ship's mast looming out of the haze some distance ahead. Carse swung *Krait* through 180 degrees, pushing the engine to full revs in the hope of not having been sighted. There was momentary apprehension when they thought that the game was up, but Berryman's eagle eye detected that the mast was from a sunken ship, and not a ship that was bearing down on them. The mast was in fact that of the wreck of *Kuala*, poking up out of the water.

The crew, guided by Lyon, continued to search for somewhere for *Krait* to hide while the attack team was away. Charts were once again studied and terrains scanned. There appeared to be nowhere obvious where the small ship could hide and be out of sight from sea level and aerial observation, and it became clear that such a hidden anchorage could take months to find. It was time they frankly did not have.

As the sun set, tensions suddenly increased when searchlights were seen sweeping at sea level to the south of them and over the stern of *Krait*. Lyon and Davidson speculated about three aircraft they had seen earlier, which had descended to 100 feet and flown away from *Krait*, presumably because they had seen the Japanese flag. However, they were now concerned that the planes may have reported *Krait* and the Japanese were looking for them. They also spotted a lone searchlight sweeping the ocean, out of range of *Krait*, but which was soon joined by a second, cranking up the tension of those on board. The only good news was that two severe tropical rainstorms had fully replenished their drinking water supplies, and the crew had taken the opportunity to strip, share a bar of soap and have a good scrub.

The log entry for 18 September noted that,

'all the crew are feeling the strain of long hours and ceaseless watching. Unless we get a quiet time soon, I will have to issue Benzedrine.'

Military instructions stated that Benzedrine, an amphetamine, may be used by personnel under severe conditions to stay alert and keep fighting for longer periods. It was only to be administered in exceptional circumstances and was used during the Allied invasion of Europe in June 1944, to boost soldiers' courage. A similar drug was widely used by German forces, called Pervitin. Benzedrine and cyanide tablets were carried on *Krait,* the latter to be used if capture were imminent. Benzedrine could only be issued with the sanction of Lyon, as Jaywick's commander, or by Carse, once the folboat crews had departed.

As they were now entering a new stage of the mission, where the enemy could become far more inquisitive, Lyon ordered only those with essential and official tasks to go on deck. To add to their apprehension, Lyon became apoplectic when it was reported that the lookout had lost a towel and hat overboard. He immediately ordered *Krait* to go back and search for the missing items, which were fortunately retrieved. 'Had the enemy found them, we would have been finished,' he shouted.

After a fruitless search for a better anchorage, Lyon decided to turn back to Pompong and anchor in a cove overnight on the opposite side of the island, away from the prying eyes of the fishing vessels. That evening, the crew set about readying *Krait* for the next stage of the mission. The mast was lowered to reduce the ship's profile. Skin dye was reapplied by crew in pairs to assist each other in the harder to reach places. This task was invariably accompanied by blaspheming and threats of physical violence, and always had Paddy McDowell in fits of laughter. He, of course, didn't have to join in, as he was always below deck lovingly caring for his engine, dressed in his overalls. With the dye applied, the folboats were carefully checked and weapons and ammunition loaded.

The night was a restless one, as the crew went over their individual responsibilities and plans repeatedly in their heads. So long in the planning, they were finally on the verge of launching the attack that Lyon had dreamt of. While he knew he could not have a finer or better trained bunch of people to do the job, he also had concerns over *Krait* being able to keep out of sight and to go unchallenged by the Japanese. The danger posed to the attack teams was extreme, but he did not underestimate the pressure for those left on board the ship, which he had decided must cruise aimlessly about, trying to remain inconspicuous – no easy task deep in enemy territory and so close to Japanese-occupied Singapore.

Next morning, they woke early at 0430 hours to the sound of engines being revved up, coming from the direction of Tjempah (now Cempah) Island, where the Japanese had set up a flying boat base. With tensions rising, everyone scanned the horizon looking for any sign of the enemy, natives or fishermen, who might give *Krait* away. The lookout spotted a small kolek, or canoe, with what looked like a Malay father and two young sons paddling towards them. Lyon could see immediately that they were on course to come within 100 metres of *Krait*. Morris was horrified when Lyon announced that they would have to kill the family, as it looked like they were going to compromise the mission.

A hurried exchange with Davidson saw the anchor weighed, as McDowell fired up the engine. Lyon then ordered Carse to sail due north, away from the approaching Malays. As the crew huddled under the awning, Morris remarked that 'those poor Malays will never know how close they came to a premature death'. Having watched Lyon in action on Durian Island, caring for terribly injured people and taking time out to bury decently those who had not survived, Morris knew that Lyon was a compassionate and honourable man. However, he also knew, better than most, that Lyon would allow nothing to put the lives of the crew at risk and would do what needed to be done to avoid compromising the mission.

They had not intended to leave Pompong Island until late afternoon, which would see them arriving at Durian in the dark. Instead, they idled among the islands south of Galang and northwest of Temiang. In mid-afternoon, while Lyon was scanning Galang Island with field glasses, he spotted a fine colonial planter's house on a hillside. More sinisterly, he noticed that behind it was what appeared to be a newly constructed Japanese watchtower. Lyon and Davidson immediately ordered the crew to stay low, with only the nominated crew members to appear on deck, while maintaining their course, as any extreme deviation could give them away to Japanese observers manning the tower.

Lyon then ordered Carse to alter course slightly, towards Kapala Jernith and Bulan Islands, in the hope that observers would assume that *Krait* was sailing to Singapore and therefore not arouse suspicion. Had Lyon not spotted the tower, they would have turned 90 degrees to port and headed west, straight towards Citlim Island and onto Durian.

The plan was now in a state of flux. Islands that had until recently been uninhabited were no longer unoccupied and seemed to be enemy outposts. Lyon was concerned that Durian would now be similarly occupied, and could simply not risk putting the folboat crews ashore as, if the island were in enemy hands, it would be tantamount to suicide. Using his local knowledge, he decided to head to Panjang Island, where the attack teams could offload their folboats and gear and hide overnight in the mangroves.

Carse, who was feeling the strain, recorded,

I won't be sorry when this day is over, as we seem to have run into a hotspot. Some two hours later he added,

We have been zig-zagging and zig-zagging all day long, from one deserted looking spot to another, only to find that we are approaching a worse one. Out of the frying pan and into the fire would be appropriate, but it does the system no good.

By 1730 hours, they were just 27 nautical miles from Singapore and praying for darkness, when Davidson called the crew to battle stations. A large naval-type craft had come out of a kampong three miles away and was heading towards them. Lyon altered course immediately. By 1935 hours, now in merciful darkness, the crew members looked north and were astonished at the glow of the lights in the sky, just 22 miles away. Lyon, who had held his steely nerve all day, calmly said, 'Welcome back, Taffy.' Morris gave him both a nervous and encouraging smile and started to sing, 'Some talk of Alexander and some of Hercules', the opening words of his old standby, 'British Grenadiers'. Everyone now understood what that meant.

The day, which felt like it would never end, still continued to be frustrating. Finally arriving at Panjang at 2200 hours, they tried to anchor but the water was too rough. They then went back out to sea, sailing slowly in circles, until finally managing to anchor until, by 0200 hours, the strong sou'-westerly wind that had made any attempt of landing impossible, finally abated sufficiently to start ferrying crew and equipment ashore.

With the gear, explosives and supplies finally transported to the beach, Morris and the others returned to *Krait*, leaving Lyon, Davidson, Page, Huston, Jones and Falls standing on the beach. Their next task would be to strike at Singapore – the heart of the hitherto invincible Japanese Empire's Jewel in the Crown.

Chapter Nine

Survive and Attack

Krait weighed anchor at 0445 hours, and Carse set about retracing their steps, avoiding the enemy bases and observation posts. As the designated reservists, Berryman and Marsh looked back at the raiding party standing on the beach with pain and a burning disappointment, as they had trained long and hard. They and *Krait* now had two long weeks to spend in waters 1000 miles behind enemy lines, unobserved. Carse, whose eyes were still affected by the glare, thought the pressure on the crew was going to be unbearable, if the next 14 days were anything like today. To add to his problems, Carse was unable to navigate using the sextant, due to the deterioration of his eyes.

Morris observed that Operation Jaywick effectively had now been split into two parts, survive and attack. The odds for the folboat crews and those who remained on *Krait* were not good. This was the unspoken truth. The next time *Krait*'s crew would meet the attack teams, if they were successful and evaded detection, would be 1 October on Pompong Island, over 100 kilometres south of Singapore. Would they make it? Morris had experienced the confusing labyrinth of islands off Singapore's coastline and had seen for himself the ruthlessness and carnage exacted by the Japanese on those trying to flee. However he did not share any of these thoughts, as he realised it would have a terrible impact on morale.

As *Krait*'s familiar silhouette slowly disappeared into the night, the attack parties also wondered when and if they would ever see their companions again. Lyon and Davidson had both expressed concerns over the depleted and young crew left on *Krait*. *If they ran into the enemy, how would they cope?* The weather, as they had already discovered, was highly unpredictable. Carse, who was older, now had to lead these young men while his eyesight was failing, and there was the unspoken potential problem of the temporary fix on the drive shaft. If *Krait* could not return for the rendezvous, the attack teams would need to try to make their way to India, the closest Allied territory. Lyon had given orders that, if they did not return to Pompong on 1 October, Carse was to set sail for Australia immediately.

Back on the beach on Panjang Island, six lonely figures set about stowing all their equipment away from the shoreline. Lyon's original assumption was that the island would be uninhabited but, as he had discovered, many of the islands now had new settlements and fishing boats operating from them. He believed this migration was an attempt by local people to distance themselves from areas occupied by the Japanese, but it would not be until daybreak that they could determine if they had any company.

As the six men finally lay down and stared up into the sky, through the canopy of the 20-metre ficus trees, Davidson felt particularly happy to be back in the jungle – his natural home, which he had come to love – and out of the swinging hammocks on *Krait*. The scuttling hermit crabs, the gentle sounds of the leaves and the cacophony of insect noises was a symphony to him. Despite the potential danger, he slept soundly that night.

The following day, 18 September, they awoke to the sound of otters chirping, purring, and squealing as they played in a rocky freshwater pool nearby. The men, highly trained in the art of killing, suddenly became childlike, transfixed by the innocent and playfulness of such beautiful creatures. After being woken in such a gentle fashion, they returned to reality and set about a reconnaissance of the island. Lyon was pleased that all their footprints from the activities of the night before had been erased by the incoming tide and hermit crabs.

Davidson established that there was a native kampong on the other side of the island, about a kilometre away, but saw no signs of tracks indicating that anyone had ventured to this side of the island. With some relief, the teams set about hiding essential provisions to be used on their return journey, enough to enable the crews to survive for one month, if needed. This was no easy task, but they eventually discovered a place to their south, high above the rocky beach and overlooking the sea. Getting the stores up there proved challenging, and it was clear that their fitness had suffered from being cooped up on *Krait* for so long.

Having completed this quite arduous task and carefully covering their tracks, Davidson insisted that over the next two days they should all try to rest and regain their strength. They also needed time to defuse the extreme tension of the last couple of days, clearing their heads to focus on the objective ahead. Lyon watched his carefully selected team swimming in the ocean, bathing, and joyfully cleaning their teeth in the freshwater pool, which always involved in horseplay and banter. He had every confidence in their abilities and the preparation undertaken to tackle the task ahead of them.

Davidson continued to display enthusiasm, energy and creativity, in the face of possible adversity. Page was calm, loyal, and highly respected. Falls had the looks and physique of an Olympian, alert and endlessly energetic. Jones was lithe of limb but, if in a scrap, a good man to have by one's side. Finally, fresh-faced Huston, the youngest member of the crew, a determined and highly motivated individual for one so young. Lyon's thoughts, which were invariably very difficult to read, were also with *Krait* and its crew and how they would evade the enemy and survive in such densely infiltrated waters.

The day of departure, 20 September, was very busy, as the attack team focused on making sure they had removed all signs of their presence, meticulously burying cans and covering footprints. They also double checked the equipment they had to load onto the folboats. It amounted to almost one-third of a ton for each boat and included limpet mines, specialist black clothing, mosquito nets,

1000 rounds of ammunition, hand guns, water and rations, vitamins, weapons such as rubber coshes and bladed knuckledusters, solid fuel cookers, sheath knives, first aid kits, charts and compass, and the vital hold-fasts required to attach the deadly limpet mines. In addition, Lyon carried the long-range telescope delivered with the extra stores to Potshot. All members of Jaywick, including those on *Krait,* had been issued with an 'L pill' – a small Bakelite container holding a lethal cyanide tablet. They had all been drilled that capture was to be avoided at all costs. For such a blatant act, their suffering at the hands of the Japanese would be unimaginable.

As they awaited nightfall, the three crews set about assembling the folboats, a task they could now do blindfolded. In final preparation they blackened their hands and faces and donned black specialist clothing, before making their way to the shoreline, carefully covering their footprints. Then, in the near distance, they heard the thrum of a powerful engine. By the sound, they determined it was far too powerful to be a local merchant or fishing vessel, and Davidson identified it as a Japanese naval launch. They then spotted the boat, moving away from them towards the southeast and, as it did so, the noise of its engines decreased.

At approximately 1900 hours they entered the water with Davidson and Falls in the lead, Lyon and Huston following five metres astern, with Page and Jones bringing up the rear. The folboats seemed dangerously low in the water, but the crews made sure they had tightened the watertight aprons around their waists as they paddled into a slight swell.

They managed to progress at a rate of just over two nautical miles per hour, stopping every hour for some chocolate, a drink of water and a quiet chat. During this time Lyon shared something they had not thought of – their compasses didn't work due to the powerful magnets in the limpet mines. However this was not to be a problem as Lyon was more than capable of navigating by the stars and, by midnight, they had covered an incredible 12 miles. Exhausted, they dragged the canoes onto the beach on Bulat Island, which they had seen during *Krait*'s reconnaissance voyage, and knew would make a reasonably safe stopover point. From here they would paddle north-west for 15 miles through the very narrow passage separating the islands of Bulan and Batam.

Waking early next morning, they were moving the canoes to a more discreet position when they heard the sound of an engine. A horrified look came over Davidson's face as he spotted a sampan with the Japanese flag flying from the stern. He reckoned it was a mere 200 metres away and was astonished that they had not been spotted. Lying low to avoid creating any profile, the teams could clearly hear men enjoying a lengthy and, what appeared to be, enjoyable breakfast. They remained in a state of paralysis for almost an hour, until the engine started and the craft moved away and eventually disappeared. Davidson, always tough on himself as well as others, scolded himself and stated that, no matter how tired they were, before going to sleep they must always ensure that they and their equipment were fully hidden. To add to the tension, a kolek with a single fisherman was now heading towards them. Luckily, he diverted towards another island, thereby preventing his inevitable and rapid demise.

For the remainder of the day the crews swam in the warm sea and relaxed. They had noticed that, the nearer they got to Singapore, the busier it became. The narrow passages between the islands forced them to make large deviations in their course to avoid detection, as it was impossible to tell the difference between a naval and merchant vessel from a distance. They also became caught in one of the tidal surges, common between the islands, which caused both Lyon's and Page's boats to lose control and plough into each other. Lyon thought that their folboat, which almost capsized, was damaged but not punctured, and was thankful it was still afloat. Spars were replaced the following day but the craft for some unknown reason did not perform in the same way, making headway more difficult.

They finally decided to stop on Bulan Island, which was not ideal as the mangroves, while providing good cover, were mosquito infested. They also discovered they were very close to a kampong and had to whisper and remain incredibly still. Luckily, a monsoonal downpour allowed them to replenish fresh water supplies and go undetected, due to the pounding noise of the tropical rainstorm. When they finally departed on 22 September, the tide in the Bulan Strait seemed kinder than previously. Even though they had experienced some mishaps, they were in fact ahead of schedule, having pushed the boundaries of human endurance, with just two hours' sleep in the past two days.

They were now four days from the planned attack. By approximately 2030 hours, they were at the north-western reaches of Batam Island. The channel was wide, which at least felt safer, and the tide had become slack. The three crews cautiously entered the Straits of Singapore, turning to starboard. When the small island, chosen as a vantage point from which to view Singapore Harbour, proved to be unsuitable, they proceeded to Dongas Island, some 9 miles distant, which Lyon knew to be a good hideaway from his sailing days.

They headed east, towards the old Dutch oil depot on Sambu Island, which Lyon had sailed past on many occasions. It was astonishingly brightly lit and looked to be working flat out. They were now 14 miles from the citadel of Singapore. The operatives looked on in awe. From their folboats, low on the water, they could only see three miles to the horizon but, while they could not see any buildings, they could see the warm glow of lights in the sky. As they had observed from the deck of *Krait*, Singapore was brightly lit. While this would create a hazard when they eventually moved in for the attack, the Japanese, it seemed, felt they had nothing to fear, so far from Allied territory and the range of any bombers. Lyon quietly smiled. They were on the threshold of achieving what had been in the planning for so long.

The journey to Dongas took almost four hours and, on approaching the island, they encountered hazardous waters with currents and sharp rocks, a potential danger to the flimsy folboats. As Lyon had suspected, Dongas was totally uninhabited, apart from some very large and colourful iguanas. There was no natural fresh water, though, as there had been on Panjang Island, but they did find a well and, while they drank the water with some apprehension, it had no ill effects.

Climbing to the highest point on the island, Lyon tied a rope to a tree and placed a clove hitch knot around the long scope to give him a steady view. He marvelled at what he saw. Dongas overlooked the Eastern Roads and, in clear visibility, Keppel Harbour and Singapore itself. He could discern his old workplace at SOE Headquarters in the Cathay Building, and Raffles Hotel, which had been the bastion of Colonial Singapore.

Lyon's surveying potential targets in Singapore harbour

He also noted that, since his hasty retreat, the skyline had changed. The old Paya Lebar wireless station had a single mast on its roof, as did the Cathay Building and there was also a signal station on St John's Island. Clearly, the Japanese had increased capacity considerably for radio traffic between Singapore and Tokyo. Lyon wondered how quickly they could communicate if the attack were successful. He could also not help but wonder if, and how, the enemy had set about using and utilising their captured facilities.

Keppel Harbour seemed to be an excellent target, and he would keep a good eye on its comings and goings. While it had not been pre-planned, Dongas also appeared to be an ideal location from which to mount their attack. As Davidson and Lyon studiously monitored the coming and goings from the harbour until 2300 hours, they saw that searchlights were scanning the night sky above the city, but there was no blackout.

Little could Lyon know that, to the east of Singapore, the Changi Peninsula was a huge prison camp, from which Allied prisoners had been sent as slave labourers to work on infamous projects such as the Thai-Burma railway. Nor did he realise that thousands of other malnourished troops were being used as slaves on the island, loading ships with rubber, copra and scrap metal, all destined to maintain the Japanese war effort.

Resuming their watch the following day, 24 September, they noted greatly increased maritime activity around Keppel Harbour. This gave the crews some relief, as the free movement of ships and vessels meant that the Japanese had not laid any mines. Lyon and Davidson agreed that, while they would maintain absolute vigilance in the execution of the mission, their observations from Dongas confirmed that the occupying Japanese forces had an air of complacency about any possible attack.

Jaywick's zero hour was still 48 hours away. However, that afternoon Davidson and Lyon estimated that in the Eastern Roads there were at least 65000 tons of enemy shipping, a most tempting target and ripe for the plucking. It was too good to miss, and they agreed that tonight was the night. Calmly, they informed the others, who welcomed the early release from the tension of waiting for the attack.

Just before dusk Lyon mustered the crews for a final briefing, assuring them that the mission had a good chance of success. Nevertheless, he also instructed them to check they could easily access the small glass vials containing the cyanide, reinforcing the point previously made to them, and their shipmates on *Krait*, that capture was not an option. However, the officers were also aware that, if captured, the crew might hesitate to crush the glass vials between their teeth, resulting in their instantaneous death. Should this be the case and capture became inevitable, the officers intended to shoot the men and then themselves.

In the tropics, darkness falls suddenly, like switching off a light. They waited until 2000 hours when, with the night enveloping them in inky blackness, they bid each other goodbye and good hunting and took to the water in their usual formation. However, although they started off well enough, powerful swirling currents forced their folboats from the intended direction. As hard as they tried, the small craft were standing still. Things were not looking good and, as they struggled to make any headway and with their energy sapping, they knew that time was running out. After five hours of futile paddling, Lyon ordered them to return to Dongas. In doing so, he was fully aware of the devastating effect it could have on morale.

The currents did not abate on the return journey, and the crews became separated, with Lyon and Huston falling behind. Their folboat was still not behaving well and it veered unpredictably, requiring more paddle power to keep it on course. Davidson, Falls, Page and Jones made it to the designated landing ground on Dongas, but Lyon and Huston did not reach land until daybreak. They thought they were on another island but could not determine where. They had, in fact, landed on the opposite side of Dongas. Both in an extremely fatigued state, they scrambled to hide their equipment and literally collapsed, lying amongst the rocks to sleep while it rained incessantly. At nightfall, the two paddled off and soon realised they were actually on Dongas. Making their way to the other side of the island, they landed and reunited with the other crew members. That evening they all enjoyed a hot and nourishing meal.

The time taken to get back to Dongas confirmed that the decision to cancel the attack had been correct. To have dallied would have seen them caught in daylight on the return journey, spelling immediate capture. With any attack from Dongas on the shipping in the Roads not viable, Lyon decided to move to a new vantage point on Subar Island, which was much nearer to their originally planned target area, being just five miles south of the Western Anchorage and the approach to Keppel Harbour. After a short period of rest, they set off in a westerly direction. Thankfully, the tides that night were more forgiving.

While Subar was not ideal for a prolonged occupation, as it offered little cover or shade and was extremely hot, it was a superb observation post. Through his telescope, Lyon identified ten ships at anchor in and around the harbour area, nine of which he assigned to each team as a designated target. It was now 26 September. Unless they made their attack that night, they would have insufficient time to get back and make a rendezvous with *Krait* on 1 October. After getting some sleep, they met to discuss the plan of action. Shortly after night fell they set off once more – this time, though, it would be their last chance.

The folboats glided silently through the night, towards the lights of Singapore, moving as swiftly as they could, with Davidson and Falls setting a tough pace at the lead. They were now halfway to the target area and the adrenaline was pounding, which helped drive them on towards their targets. Suddenly, a searchlight hit them, almost like a projectile. Davidson thought it was coming from the top of the Cathay Building. To the crew's great credit and discipline, on Lyon's order they calmly turned the bows of their folboats through 90 degrees to starboard and pointed them straight to the source of illumination. They had practised for such an eventuality many times at Camp X, knowing that it reduced their signature on the surface of the water dramatically. Feeling that the game was well and truly up, the men froze. As the searchlight fixed on the folboats, they fully expected that other lights scanning the sky and approaches would also hone in on them. Capture seemed inevitable, but Davidson thought at least they would have time to take their cyanide capsules before their captors got to them and delivered them into the hands of the dreaded Kempeitai or secret police. However, after 30 seconds, which seemed like an eternity, the light went out.

Davidson and Falls split from the other two teams to target the inner harbour, narrowly avoiding being obliterated by a fast-moving steam tug. Not relishing the thought of being shredded by its powerful churning propeller and barnacled bottom, they wrestled with their canoe in an attempt to avoid what they thought would be certain death. However, at the last minute it turned to head off for Blakang Mati Island, leaving the two men alive but badly shaken.

That danger over, they kept an eye on a searchlight sweeping across to the west. Arriving at Keppel Harbour, their target destination, they were surprised to find it mysteriously empty. As the nearby Empire Docks were too well lit, they proceeded east to the Roads, where there were still plenty of ships. Davidson identified three cargo vessels, two heavily laden, which he estimated to be 6000 tons each. Approaching the targets from the port side, away from the lights of Singapore, they drifted with the tide and began the process of attaching the limpets.

Although they had rehearsed this procedure many times on Australian navy ships, the clang as the magnetic mine attached itself to the hull was extremely unnerving. Nevertheless, with surgical precision they attached the rest of the limpets and set the fuses for a seven-hour delay. A distant clock chimed one in the morning, which was their signal to beat a hasty retreat. The job complete, they set off for the Riau Straits and Batam Island, their rate of speed noticeably faster with the folboat relieved from the weight of the limpets, as they strove to put as much distance between themselves and Singapore.

Lyon and Huston had progressed further to the west to Examination Anchorage, but were unable to find their ships, due to the total darkness. Eventually they found a large oil tanker, a target usually avoided as it was more difficult to sink or damage, due to its multi-compartments. The vessel, believed to be *Shosei Maru*, was formerly *Solen*, a British oil tanker of 8500 tons, abandoned in Singapore by her crew on 15 February 1942 and seized by the Japanese. In an attempt to maximise the damage, the pair decided to place all nine limpets on the hull. As they moved along the side of the ship, carefully linking the charges, Huston glanced up. Looking down, from a porthole just three metres above his head, was a Japanese seaman. Huston froze. In the dark it was difficult to discern if he had actually seen them, but shortly afterwards he withdrew his head and his cabin light came on, rattling both Lyon and Huston. Hoping that their presence was not being reported to the ship's watch officer, they finished their task and sped off for Dongas Island, over three hours' paddle away.

At 2200 hours Page and Jones stealthily approached Bukom Island, an oil depot almost directly opposite Labrador Battery. The area was brightly lit and, as they came closer, they could not help but feel the danger, as they could see many Japanese guards and naval personnel. However, aided by their low profile and black camouflage they proceeded silently towards their prey undetected, and cruised around for almost 60 minutes, choosing their prizes. The first was a freighter, which they approached from the stern, attaching the limpets fore and aft. By 2300 hours, however, they could feel the tide turning, which this time was in their favour as it delivered them to their next target, *Nasusan Maru*, a converted tanker. Moving into the area where ships were being repaired and welded, they identified their third and final target – an old and extremely vulnerable looking rusting freighter, which Page thought would sink easily. Moving alongside they attached the limpet to the holdfast and carefully placed it below the waterline. This time, there was no reassuring clang as the magnet made contact with the hull. At first they thought it must be faulty but then quickly realised that the freighter was literally a floating rust bucket. Jones carefully and quietly scraped away the rust until each limpet attached itself with a satisfyingly reassuring clang. With that, they departed.

Page and Jones made for Dongas Island, arriving 30 minutes ahead of an extremely fatigued Lyon and Huston, who had been wrestling with their capricious folboat. Deep in the mangroves, as they exchanged exciting accounts of their collective successful deployments, pre-dawn darkness erupted with explosions and deep thunderous thuds echoing across the Straits. Suddenly, the lights of the city went out.

As sirens wailed, Lyon, Huston, Page, and Jones shook hands and allowed themselves a brief moment of satisfaction and relief, which had been a long time coming. They were, though, still in extreme danger and had a very long way to go until they would reach anything like safety. The four men set off scrambling through the undergrowth for the high ground on Dongas. As dawn was breaking, Lyon once again used his telescope to review the damage they had wreaked, before moving aside to allow the others to try to spot their victims. While some were obvious, positive sightings were difficult due to orders obviously issued for all vessels to be put to sea. Lyon thought the Japanese had ordered the ships out of their moorings and into the Straits, as the source of the danger had not been identified. Vessels of all types were now steaming up and down the Straits, blocking a clear view from Dongas. Lyon could, however, see the hull of a sunken ship sticking up out of the water. Also, the tanker he and Huston had chosen as their victim was clearly ablaze, and the fire showed no sign of being extinguished. The attack had had the desired effect – mass panic, and a greatly heightened feeling of vulnerability.

Shortly after 0600 hours, a twin-engined aircraft took off from Kallang airfield, in the east, heading west in the direction of the Malacca Straits. Other aircraft that had taken off returned at around 0800 hours, before once again taking off and flying directly over Dongas Island, before heading off and searching around the southern islands at low level.

From the clouds of smoke billowing from Singapore harbour and the resultant chaos that was ensuing, the raid was classed as an undoubted success. It was estimated that seven enemy ships, totalling 37,000-39,000 tons, had been sunk or damaged. Several Japanese signals, intercepted and decoded by United States intelligence, revealed that ships were damaged in Singapore Harbour in the early morning of 27 September 1943, with holes about two metres wide blown in their sides.

Chapter Ten

Rendezvous Pompong

Lyon, Huston, Page and Jones lay low and rested on Dongas Island for the whole of 27 September, while Davidson and Falls rested among the thick undergrowth and mangroves on a small island off the north-easterly tip of Batam Island. However, with things hotting up, Davidson and Falls decided to put more distance between themselves and the enemy, and ploughed on, proceeding south through the Riau Straits for Pandjang Island, with several stops along the way. The route was heavy with local native traffic, and more than once they were spotted by native fishermen. The plan was to go ahead and make the rendezvous with *Krait* on Pompong on the deadline of 1 October, as Lyon was expecting his voyage with the troublesome folboat to take a little longer.

On 29 September, after a marathon two-day paddle, Davidson and Falls reached Otter Bay on Pandjang where, after their arduous trip, they tucked into the food they had left behind in the cliff-face dump. As the others also planned to stop at Pandjang, Davidson scribbled a note to Lyon, which he left among the rest of the stores, telling him that they had arrived safely and were on schedule for the final rendezvous.

As soon as day turned to night, the two continued on the 50-kilometre journey south-east to Pompong. Two hours into their journey they were engulfed by a severe storm that seemed to come out of nowhere. Known as 'Sumatra Squall Lines', they occur when air pressure, developed over Sumatra at night, whips up severe winds and seas and blows eastwards towards the Malay peninsula. Many vessels and sailors had met their maker due to this destructive natural phenomenon.

Davidson and Falls were now forced to battle the elements for a further two long hours, battered by a head-on wind, spray, and mountainous seas. The lightning strikes were white flashes that came out of total darkness, blinding them for minutes on end. Eventually, they found some shelter just before daybreak, at Abang Besar Island, about halfway to Pompong Island. Shaken and fatigued, they hid their folboat and fell soundly asleep.

Meanwhile, the two other canoes had arrived at Otter Bay during another severe Sumatra squall early that morning. After hiding their folboats and gear and preparing a meal, they hid throughout the daylight hours to get some rest before completing the final leg to Pompong.

On Abang Besar, Davidson and Falls – now rested – prepared for the last part of the journey to where they would hopefully rendezvous with *Krait*. As always, at around 1900 hours, day suddenly became night, giving Davidson and Falls twelve hours of darkness to get to Pompong. Departing Abang Besar, they headed further to the south-east, with strong currents tugging at their folboat. This time, though, they would prevail, and made good steady progress to arrive at Pompong at 0100 hours, averaging 2.5 miles per hour since their departure, a significantly faster pace than the inward journey. They hid their folboat in the trees in a small bay on the quieter, western side of Pompong, where they were less likely to be seen by inquisitive eyes, and hung their wet gear out to dry.

Davidson was worried about the other two teams, not seen since leaving Subar to carry out the attack. He was also concerned about *Krait* and her crew, dodging, hiding, and moving among the islands while not attracting attention or suspicion. Looking out across the narrow stretch of water between the much larger Bakung Island and Pompong, Davidson surveyed the passage to the south-east and then to the north-west, wondering which approach *Krait* would take. After discussing the matter with Falls, the pair decided that at dusk, some ten hours away, they would paddle around the island to look for *Krait*. That night, with great expectation, they slipped the folboat into the water and set off in search of shipmates they had not seen for almost two weeks. After slowly lapping the island for several hours and scanning the horizon, their hopes of a sighting faded.

Heading back to their hideout in a subdued mood, they hid the folboat in the trees and tried to get some sleep. That evening, they circled the island once more and listened intently for the gentle throb of *Krait*'s silenced exhaust. Then, shortly after midnight on 2 October, a familiar silhouette appeared. With renewed enthusiasm and excitement, they paddled out towards the ship, where they were spotted by the crew on watch.

The mood on *Krait*, which had been very tense in recent days, was immediately lifted with Davidson's larger than life personality back on board. Questions were fired from every direction, and Davidson had to calm everyone down, such was the excitement and noise generated by the reunion. As soon as the folboat team boarded *Krait*, Crilly had gone below to warm a special meal that he had prepared for six – not two. As *Krait*'s crew had been expecting the other two teams to also arrive, Davidson painted a positive picture, but the strain and anxiety regarding their well being could be seen in everyone's eyes.

Many of *Krait*'s crew were offering up private prayers, in the knowledge that Davidson and Falls had not actually seen the others since leaving Subar Island. When Morris, who was particularly concerned, asked 'Are Major Lyon and the others going to make it?', Davidson explained that he had left the note on Panjang Island, and that Lyon's and Huston's canoe had been damaged.

Meanwhile, Page and Jones were the first to leave Panjang, one hour ahead of Lyon and Huston. While it was a risk, they paddled throughout the day in order to attempt the rendezvous and to explain that Lyon and Huston, battling with their damaged folboat, were definitely on their way. Lyon and Huston literally wrestled with their folboat with every stroke of the paddles, but sheer determination drove them on, with the two crews arriving at

Pompong at the same time, at 0400 hours. Circling the island and scanning the horizon, they could see no sign of *Krait*.

Had the ship left without them? With tired muscles and heavy hearts, they hid their folboats and took shelter, all resting up for the day.

As Lyon was well aware of his instructions for *Krait* to sail for Australia if anyone missed the rendezvous, he was already planning for a prolonged stay on Pompong, with a view to seizing a local vessel and sailing it to India. However, they woke just before nightfall on October 2 to see *Krait* sailing away from them, heading south. Following up on this massive disappointment, the crews saw signs that Davidson and Falls had recently been on the island, lifting their spirits, as they knew Davidson would explain the reason for their delay.

On his return to the ship, Davidson soon found that understandably Carse's and the crews nerves had become particularly frayed. The tension became heightened when Davidson communicated with Carse very directly and essentially ordered him to not to obey Lyon's order to sail for Australia should they miss the rendezvous. Carse initially insisted on obeying Lyon's command. The very direct instruction delivered by Davidson and the manner in which it was delivered saw Carse accede to Davidson's instruction. The build up and strain of this period was reflected in the log book entry,

'We are all filled with anxiety, as we have had no news at all of the party and this does not seem too good to us' and when Krait eventually set course to make the rendezvous, *'Anxiety remains, however, as we do not know if we are walking into a trap or not.'*

Even though tensions understandably had steadily built during the past fortnight, the crew had somehow continued to work well together with Crilly, as usual, achieving the impossible in preparing tasty food from some wholly unappetising rations. In the engine room McDowell had been kept busy, nursing the engine and praying every day that the shaft would stay intact. Morris was his usual reassuring self, singing a tailored song or ballad to fit the mood. Cain had ensured his repertoire of jokes were frequently delivered, which undoubtedly helped keep morale up and to maintain their nerve in that very tense period. When Davidson read *Krait*'s log, he saw how the pressure on board had been brought to a peak, with an entry penned by Carse, dated 29 September,

'In future operations, it would be better if the crew were older than say 25. The younger members do not seem to realise their responsibilities as they should and have been told continuously to do ordinary routine duties. Unless told daily, their arms are never cleaned, and on watch they tend to become slack. A cruise like this does not seem to provide them with the excitement they crave. A fight with a patrol boat would not find them wanting, but might prove fatal to the result of this cruise. I hope that now I have fully awakened them to their responsibilities. If I have not succeeded in doing so, the fault is their own stupidity and carelessness.'

2 October log entry continued,

'We lay at anchor till daybreak but no sign of the others. As we are directly under a well-travelled plane route, we weighed at 06.15 and proceeded down Temiang Strait. We will then set a course E by S and return again tonight. It seems that Major Lyon is feeling the strain and as his partner a/A.B. Huston is the weakest link in the chain he might find some difficulty in getting back. Sleep is the main need of all hands at present. While trying to break the anchor from the ground this morning, the hawser parted. It had been frayed by the heavy tide rips during the night. So now we have no anchor large enough to hold the ship in a big swell. This means that we will have to cruise around all night tonight. As daylight tomorrow is the deadline for waiting if they are not there tonight we wont know what to do. The major

said that if still alive by then they would concentrate on taking a sailing vessel and making their way back that way. If he can't make it tonight, it would be better to send Lt Page and a/A.B. Jones back to us to act as guides for us to pick them up at an advanced rendezvous. However we will have to await the night and see what it will bring. I am too tired to sleep and the dye has brought out a sort of rash which is itching like hell. There is no wind and it is one of those hot sticky days when it is uncomfortable any way you sit or lie or stand. The temperature is 92 degrees on deck and 130 degrees in the engine room. We are just cruising around the China Sea waiting for dark and praying for better visibility than we had last night for our passage through the strait. Had the Japs been at all considerate they would have erected a few lights at the danger spots to facilitate our passages. After consideration it has been decided to postpone our re-entry into Temiang till tomorrow afternoon. This means that they will have two nights for travel instead of one and if we get there at dusk they will not have shifted as they only travel at night. If they are not there we will run onto Panjang and see if they have received a message Lt Davidson left for them. If they have not reached Panjang by then we will, I am afraid, have to give them up for lost.'

Back on Pompong, Lyon wasted no time in putting his team to work, finding water supplies and building a shelter while he arranged with a local fisherman to keep them supplied with food. Having a plan and securing provisions had boosted their frayed morale. Now in much better shape than when they arrived on Pompong, they prepared and ate an evening meal. Then, one hour after darkness fell, they heard the unmistakable throb of *Krait*'s exhaust. Never had such a sound been so welcomed.

With everyone back on board, it felt like a coming home and a moment that no one would ever forget, as crew members excitedly exchanged their news, the success in Singapore Harbour, the storms, the near misses. One thing that puzzled them was why the Japanese search and surveillance after the attack had concentrated on the Malacca Strait, to the west of the island. Lyon believed it was because the Japanese never considered that an attack could come at all, let alone from the sea. No one was aware of the retribution that was about to unfold for Jaywick's daring attack on the Japanese Empire.

Chapter Eleven

Running the Gauntlet

With everyone back on board, Lyon ordered large tots of rum to celebrate their success and *Krait* set off on a calm sea, at long last heading home. To allow the raiding party to have a well-earned sleep, the remainder of the crew offered to keep watch, navigate, and maintain the boat. Morris noted that, while morale had been lifted by their success, everyone was very tired and jaded, and most were suffering from prickly heat, carbuncles, and boils which he did his best to treat.

At 0300 hours on 4 October, *Krait* cleared the Temiang Strait and altered course to east-south-east. At 1348 hours, the watch officer alerted the crew to a seaplane approaching overhead, heading towards *Krait* from the south. To everyone's great relief it passed over, taking no notice, and headed off in the direction of Singapore.

By daybreak on 6 October, they were sailing with excruciating slowness in a south-easterly direction, passing between Serutu and Karimata islands on their port bow and Belitung Island to their starboard. The one factor in their favour was the haze, which kept visibility in daylight to a minimum. Edging further out into the Java Sea, they passed Tanjong Sambar at around 0600 hours on October 7, while keeping a watchful eye on southern Borneo, formerly governed by the Dutch. The north, which was formerly ruled by the British, was now in the hands of the Japanese Imperial Army, while the south was under the command of the Japanese Imperial Navy – two good reasons to keep as much distance between them and *Krait* as possible. All were secretly fearful of the likelihood of being intercepted by a major Japanese warship, against which they had very little defence.

Continuing on, steering a course in mid-channel, they passed by Karimunjawa and Bawean Islands, which lie between Borneo to the north and Java to the south. As they progressed further into the voyage, *Krait*'s diesel generator was struggling to keep the batteries charged. Because of the excessive charging due to the low number of batteries on board, *Krait* was now down to her last 45-gallon drum of diesel, which had to get them back to Australia.

As the days passed by slowly, Lyon, Page and Davidson took it in turns to debrief *Krait*'s crew members, while Falls, Huston and Jones were tasked with recording, from memory, the events since they left *Krait* to undertake their attack on Singapore.

The raiders also learned how *Krait* had sailed around the Java Sea from the west coast of Borneo heading south to just beyond Galam Island, heading north-west and weaving between Pelapis Island and the mainland before heading back towards Singapore and the final rendezvous at Pompong. The notes and the detailed ship's log that Carse had been instructed to keep were carefully compared and aided greatly in helping Lyon, as Jaywick's Commanding Officer, prepare a report for his superiors.

Carse had good reason as the navigator to have openly expressed that he had a morbid fear of the Lombok Strait, which was several days' sailing away. Not only was the navigation the most difficult part of the voyage he was aware that at this point they were exposed more closely to the enemy and at risk from the rip tides. Understanding Carse's concerns and those of the crew Davidson and Lyon agreed on a strategy to ensure the navigator was effectively supported. Both understood he was not only suffering from his eye disorder, but he also had incredibly painful and inflamed elbows, and it was obvious that the voyage was taking its toll.

The plan was to work with Carse at close quarters and, as both senior officers knew that any cause for anxiety amongst the crew could be infectious, everyone was kept very busy. Carse was kept occupied by carefully studying the tide tables and the moon's meridian passage. He calculated that from 2330 hours on the night of 10-11 October, conditions would be optimal to tackle the Lombok Strait. No one wanted a repeat of their outward voyage, being caught in a riptide in total daylight, with the engine at full throttle and the ship standing still. Carse was also extremely concerned that, apart from the obvious danger of the Japanese, such a prolonged stress on the engine would shatter the temporary fix on *Krait*'s propeller shaft.

Good progress was being made when, just after nightfall on 8 October, *Krait*'s engine coughed and spluttered and the ship staggered to a halt, with the bow dipping in the water. Lyon and the remainder of the crew felt their stress levels rise, although the normally busy shipping lanes had been very quiet. Down below, Paddy McDowell could be heard cussing as the atmosphere in the engine room turned blue. The crew was highly relieved therefore, when, after what seemed an interminable time, Carse and Lyon were informed that McDowell had replaced a fractured spring on the fuel valve and, while he was at it, had also taken the opportunity to change all the lubricating oil. As the engine fired up once more, McDowell was reassured to see that the engine oil pressure gauge was perfect at 32 pounds at 8000 revolutions. It had been a tense one hour and fifteen minutes of drifting aimlessly, but at 2045 hours they resumed their southeasterly course, edging ever nearer towards the strait.

The sea and winds had reduced *Krait*'s progress to 120 miles a day, averaging five knots and, at nightfall on 9 October, the ship altered course abeam off the islands of Masalembu Besar and Masalembu Kecil, to the north of Bali and Lombok islands, approximately halfway between Borneo and the Lombok Strait. *Krait* now steered directly south, aiming to reach the entrance to the strait on the evening of 11 October, hopefully encountering favourable tides and sailing through, under the cover of nightfall. On 10 October, they were just 26 hours from the strait when the crew began to get what had become known as the 'Lombok Feeling', something that Morris did not relish. However, the weather was perfect, and Carse prayed for it to hold until they were 300 miles and three days south of the strait and out of enemy territory. His sense of foreboding was again reflected in the log,

'Our trip back so far has been quiet and it really needs to remain so as one and only one mistake means good night for us.'

On the night of 10 October, *Krait*'s engines were reduced to 6000 revolutions per minute to slow the vessel and avoid being ahead of the optimum time calculated to pass through the strait. By 1637 hours the next day, towards the south-west, they sighted the volcanic peak of Mount Agung on Bali, while Lombok's equally impressive Mount Rinjani could be viewed intermittently between the clouds that shrouded it.

Everyone set about staining their skin except for Arthur Jones, who was now of even leaner build and even more tanned, making him once more a natural deck decoy. With land now on both sides, the feeling of sailing into a bottleneck ramped up the tension and focused minds. Everyone started to whisper, although clearly no one was near to hear. Everyone was also silently praying for cloud cover, as it would be full moon that night.

The day was also the clearest they had experienced in the last week, something viewed as unfavourable, but at least the turbulent current was running with them this time. The calculations and timing were near to perfection. They had ninety minutes of daylight before they arrived at the entrance to the strait. As darkness rapidly fell, the feeling of tension was exacerbated as Carse increased the engine speed to full revs and *Krait* started to vibrate. As the water became more turbulent, it began to wash over the deck. On entering the narrowest section of the strait, exactly on schedule at 2300 hours, the water seemed to syphon and the previously agitated currents united to run in the one direction, southwards, aiding *Krait*'s progress.

So far so good, Lyon thought, as he accompanied Page below to listen with Young for transmissions alerting them to the enemy's presence. Topside, Falls and Jones were scanning the horizon, eagle-eyed for anything that moved, while Davidson was closeted with Carse in the wheelhouse, speaking to him calmly as they steadily edged forward. Then, without warning, the relative calm was broken when Falls, who was monitoring the port side from bow to stern, spotted a silhouette moving from the shore of Lombok Island. Jones immediately locked on to where his watch mate was pointing. Both struggled with their binoculars, clouded by the intense humidity. The outline was getting larger, and a bow wave became visible, which said one thing, fast moving naval vessel heading straight toward them.

'Go and tell the boss we have a problem,' Jones said to Falls. He first alerted Davidson in the wheelhouse, then proceeded to wake members of the crew who were under the awning trying to get some sleep, before going below to alert Lyon. Realising the danger, Lyon flew up onto the deck. On sighting the rapidly approaching vessel, he called all hands to action stations. This was the moment everyone had been dreading. Weapons were passed around and the awning's canvas sides lowered, allowing the crew to see through the slits. If overcome, they knew they could not be taken alive. No uniforms, no ID tags and flying the Japanese flag. Their destiny was sealed.

Lyon walked to the stern, where most of the crew were crouched under the cover of the awning, calming his men, reassuring them that they had been well rehearsed for such an eventuality. However, the plan to use a dinghy to limpet mine the enemy vessel, if *Krait* were challenged, was scrapped, as Lyon judged that it would be almost impossible to carry it out in the prevailing sea conditions, which were choppy with a fast-running southerly current.

Armed and ready to strike the crew members were determined to make a good account of themselves. As the vessel approached, Carse estimated it to be a destroyer of between 260 and 300 feet in length and recorded this in the ships log. Davidson however, using his identification manual, deduced that the silhouette was a Minesweeper. Analysis undertaken many years later would confirm Davidsons assessment at the time to have been the more accurate. The vessel had the sole duty of patrolling the Lombok Strait, and was extremely intimidating and significantly larger than *Krait*. As it loomed closer, the sense of foreboding amongst the crew grew greater. Lyon, expecting a searchlight to strike them at any moment and for the ship to be hailed by a loudspeaker, crouched down next to his old comrade, Morris, who was gripping his Sten gun in anticipation. 'How are you feeling?' Lyon asked. Morris's face said it all but he managed to smile and said, 'It's not so much how I am feeling, it's how they are feeling.' Lyon and Morris had experienced similar close scrapes during their escape from Singapore, and by some miracle had come through relatively unscathed, but some members of the crew were in their late teens and had never experienced such pressure, nor had they been exposed to armed warfare. Lyon and Morris looked at the crouched figures, who appeared almost ready to pounce. 'The lads are bearing up well,' observed the seasoned, 24-year-old Morris.

The Japanese vessel had appeared to be ready to ram *Krait* and split her in two when the Japanese helmsman swung the wheel to port, reduced throttle, and ran alongside. The crew's pumping hearts felt as if they would burst from their chests. Young, who was below, listening for any enemy radio traffic, nervously eyed the high explosive charges next to him, part of the last resort contingency plan. Davidson meanwhile set about checking the detonators that would be fired to scuttle the ship. Once the plunger was depressed, the resulting explosion would annihilate them all, leaving no trace or evidence of them, or their clandestine mission.

As the hands of the clock ticked by in what seemed to be slow motion, Carse manoeuvred *Krait* so that those on the bridge of the enemy ship had a line of sight to the bedraggled Japanese flag fluttering from the stern. The two vessels were now so close that *Krait*'s crew, peering through the slits in the awning, could easily discern the silhouettes of Japanese officers and crew on the bridge. The tension was almost unbearable. Lyon said, 'Hold your fire now, and do nothing until I tell you.' For at least five long minutes, the enemy ship ran alongside, scrutinising the supposedly harmless, dirty little fishing vessel. No searchlights appeared, there was no sound of anyone hailing, nor the thunder of a warning shot across *Krait*'s bow. Then, without any explanation, the sea at the stern of the enemy vessel appeared to boil as the engine notes increased, and she turned sharply to port and back towards Lombok. As he waited for the stern light to disappear, Lyon gestured the crew to remain absolutely still and silent.

The tension broke when Marsh calmly and casually stated, 'Thank Christ that's over'. Lyon simply patted everyone on the back, saying 'Well done, chaps', while a fraught and mentally exhausted Carse gratefully handed over his watch and his stint at the wheel to Davidson. At this point, Morris scurried down to the engine room to check on his fellow crew mate, Paddy McDowell. 'Lend me some toilet paper, Paddy,' Morris said, knowing there was no such commodity on board, as it had been banned. 'What do you want it for?' was McDowell's extremely terse reply to the ebullient Welshman. 'What do you think I want it for, after that little lot? The normally stolid McDowell cracked and burst into laughter.

Later Carse recorded these tense moments from sighting of the Japanese vessel in *Krait*'s log,

'On looking at it I saw a large naval patrol, with a bone in her teeth, approaching rapidly on our beam. All hands were called and armed and everything prepared to evacuate. We approached bows on to within about one hundred yards then slowed down and turned alongside on our port quarter. Seeing her beam on she appeared to be a modern type destroyer between 260 and 300 feet long. After pacing us for about five minutes she sheered off and went directly away from us. Although we were undoubtedly seen she did not hail or challenge us in any way neither did she use a searchlight. As she turned a light was visible aft otherwise she was in darkness. It was midnight before she was out of *sight. Whether it was because of the approach to the change of watches and the officer of the first had had a big day and wanted to go to his bunk, or they had got into trouble with some high ranking official over stopping similar boats we can't tell, but it was certainly a miracle.'*

As if they had not suffered enough, the challenges of the night were not yet over. Approaching the southern entrance to the strait two hours later the ocean appeared to boil as the tides collided. *Krait* pitched and yawed in colossal 13-metre foot waves, water pouring over her decks as the crew clung on for dear life.

The entry in the log recorded,

'the hazards of the tide rips and heavy seas seemed like sitting before a nice fire, so very little notice was taken of them when, at 0245 hrs, we struck the rips on the southern side. At 0340 hrs we passed between Nusa Besar and Lombok and, setting course due south, ran into heavy sea about 6. 0545 hrs at daylight, Nusa Besar and Telok Blongas were still visible astern and the sea still 6. Wind 4 South Easterly. Barometer 29.94. The sky was hazy with a tendency to cloud over. Well, if we survive tomorrow, all should be well, but if possible we do not want another like last night.'

At 1930 hours on 12 October, in what were thought to be waters of relative safety, Lyon ordered the Japanese ensign to be lowered. If left flying, they might now be mistaken as an enemy vessel. The following morning, at 0530 hours, Carse recorded,

'Tonight we will radio Admiral Christie of the American submarines re-patrol of the Lombok Strait. This has been arranged, and the single word POTSHOT conveys that to him. If he radios back asking after our welfare, we can give our E.T.A. If he does not, we will wait till Friday night or Saturday morning.'

In a rare moment of relief at 1800 hours on 13 October when exiting enemy controlled waters the log records,

'Spliced the main brace to celebrate our departure from the area of Japanese influence.'

The attempt to radio Darwin failed and Carse records the concern for being mistaken for an enemy vessel when he recorded in the log,

'As no-one knows our E.T.A., it might be a case of running into danger from our own batteries, as our contour has altered with the removal of our mast and our rise above sea level is now quite noticeable.'

On 14 October *Krait* was 480 miles from Exmouth Gulf and, the nearer they were, the more excited the crew became. However, as night fell they were aware that the ship's engine was playing up, which led to a tense one-and-a-half hours of aimless drifting, while an angry McDowell attempted to repair the oil cooling system. Even though they were about halfway between Bali and Exmouth, the thought of engine failure certainly put a dampener on things. Then, to everyone's great relief, the engine fired and *Krait* resumed her course southwards at a steady six knots.

The next day at 1140 hours, the lookout on *Krait* spotted a flying boat, astern and heading in a due easterly direction. As he was unable to identify if it were a friend or foe, Lyon again called the crew to action stations. After a tense ten minutes with the crew standing at arms, the unknown aircraft disappeared from sight. Ploughing on, the ship encountered difficult seas of force 4-5. Carse noted that,

'Owing to the wind and sea, the taking of sights was impossible. About six different horizons were visible and not one was the correct one.'

At 1100 hours, the crew spotted the Montebello Islands and Tryall Rocks, as Carse carefully navigated through an archipelago of 174 small islands. It was their first sighting of Australian soil and it felt like a very good omen but, 15 minutes later, *Krait* once again ground to a halt. This time McDowell diagnosed blocked fuel lines. One thing was clear – that the homeward voyage was not uneventful nor without its tensions. After 30 minutes of expletive explosions from McDowell, *Krait* once again spluttered into life and plodded on. Like a punch-drunk boxer getting up off the canvas, she staggered towards the Australian coastline, and by 1400 hours was battling a force 6 gale. The helmsman cut the engine speed to half revs but as they progressed in heavy seas towards Barrow Island, the weather worsened and reached force 7.

The ship's log recorded,

A very rough night was experienced. Many of the waves rising above 30 feet.

On 18 October the sea conditions mercifully abated as if to welcome them as they moved closer to Potshot. However, with Fly Island abeam and Eva Island on their port bow, the sea again started to churn. The log records,

Wind has now increased to gale force about 8 and the sea becoming very steep and choppy. Wind and sea were both very high taking green seas over continuously.

Krait abruptly altered course to S 40 W and reduced speed to just 500 revs, to arrive safely at Exmouth Gulf in the early hours of 19 October. At 0200 hours the anchor rattled over the side as *Krait* came to a final rest two miles east of USS *Chanticleer*. Realising that, for the first time in seven long weeks they were back on friendly territory, the sense of relief Morris and the crew experienced was almost overwhelming.

Davidson, ever the practical joker and wishing to finish the mission on a high, gathered everyone and outlined a plan of arrival to surprise the *Chanticleer*'s crew. After their best sleep since leaving Exmouth, more than six weeks before, Davidson woke the others at dawn and by 0600 hours, after a short snack of biscuits and tea, they had weighed anchor and were on their way to Potshot. Running almost silently at low revs, *Krait* pulled alongside *Chanticleer*, her low profile keeping her under the reach of radar. Climbing from the roof of *Krait*'s wheelhouse, the crew stepped over *Chanticleer*'s gunwale and onto the deck. Avoiding the guards and early risers wandering around the deck, the Jaywick men, employing the same stealth they had practised so many times before, reached the mess deck, where they gave themselves up. They were then paraded before *Chanticleer*'s Lieutenant Commander Hawes.

Looking sternly at the bedraggled group of what could best be described as mercenaries or pirates, he said, 'What the hell have we got here?

'We thought we would give you a surprise,' replied Lyon.

Finding it hard to maintain his stern façade, Hawes broke into a broad smile and welcomed them back. For the first time since early September, Corporal Crilly, who had so tirelessly slaved away in *Krait*'s galley to produce weird and wonderful dishes, enjoyed a full American breakfast, including piping hot, fresh coffee, along with the rest of the crew. However, he politely declined the offer of pancakes.

Following breakfast, Morris, who was still struggling with the unhealed wound to his ankle, clambered back onboard *Krait* and emerged from below deck with four large bottles containing a gallon of dark rum that he had accumulated and saved throughout the voyage. He was eagerly welcomed by *Chanticleer*'s alcohol starved crew members, who exchanged the rum for a sack full of American cigarettes for this very welcome imbibing liquid. Meanwhile, Lyon and Davidson set about trying to bring the crew back to normal life, with mundane matters such as the issue of new clothing and kit. They certainly needed them. No identification papers, no uniforms, just their filthy shorts and sarongs and deeply tanned and stained skins. While the crew enjoyed the luxury of steaming hot showers and enjoyed their well-earned and excellent US hospitality, Davidson soon had things sorted.

Whilst Operation Jaywick was still very much kept top-secret, congratulatory signals started to flow in, from Lord Gowrie, the Commonwealth Naval Board and from Jock Campbell at SOA

Headquarters in Melbourne. Lyon and Page also attended a dinner held in their honour, hosted by Admiral Christie Commander of the United States Pacific Submarine Operations. He had been informed of Jaywick's success by naval intelligence, and was one of the very few outsiders who knew of their mission. His boss, General MacArthur, the Supreme Commander South-West Pacific, was privately very impressed, although publicly very cool about the success of Jaywick. He still harboured deep concerns and cynicism regarding Allied intentions and plans for the former British Empire's bastion, and what he saw as attempts to reclaim the Empire. Admiral Christie, however, was of a different mindset when he recorded,

'Last night I had dinner with Major Ivan Lyon of the Gordon Highlanders and Captain Page of the Australian Army. Ivan Lyon is an extremely brave man, possibly the bravest man I have ever met. Almost a single-handed endeavour of extremely bold pattern. My hat is off to them. Someday his exploits will be disclosed, and they will read stranger than any fiction.'

However, the euphoria of Jaywick's success was dampened when Lyon received instructions that no one was to reveal any details of the mission and that severe sanctions would be brought to bear against any crew member who gave the secret away. Even though they knew they had to obey orders, Lyon and the team were perplexed, disappointed and extremely angry, as the sole objective of Operation Jaywick was one of propaganda – to strike at the heart of the Japanese Empire, with the threat of more to come. Not to be able to share their jubilation and success with the world was not only frustrating, but it was, to their minds, deeply counter-productive. Orders were orders, but Lyon was determined to get answers.

Lyon discovered that General Blamey and SOA's senior officers were responsible for the clampdown and enforced secrecy on the success of the Jaywick mission. He and Davidson were furious that the entire mission's efforts and success were wasted in not achieving a spectacular propaganda coup. While the enforced secrecy was galling, they had no idea that innocent people in Singapore, who had nothing to do with Jaywick, would pay a terrible price for the security clampdown.

The first to split from the group at Exmouth Gulf was Morris. Leaving his crew mates ashore, he waved them farewell from the deck of *Chanticleer*, bound for Fremantle, where he would receive medical attention to his ankle. After such a dangerous mission, his was the only injury incurred, and from 'friendly fire'. Morris enjoyed the company of the Americans, who knew that *Krait*'s crew had been up to something and teased him that his injury had earned him a Purple Heart – an award bestowed on US servicemen and women for meritorious service in combat. *If only they knew the full truth*, Morris thought.

The rest of the team now began to break up. Lyon and Page were flown to Melbourne for a full debriefing by SOA, while Davidson and the remaining crew, after *Krait* had received much needed repairs and overhaul, sailed to Darwin, where the ship was handed over to SOA for possible use on future missions.

Over the coming weeks, the crew were also debriefed – to some it felt like interrogation – and every detail disclosed to intelligence officers was recorded, compared, and triangulated to ensure that the information they were being given was not embellished. In Brisbane on 10 November, after some first-class medical treatment and care, Morris was reunited with his fellow crew members who had flown from Darwin the previous day. The next day, 11 November and Armistice Day, the entire Jaywick team joined Jock Campbell at a celebration party at Meigunyah House – a rambling colonial building in the suburb of Bowen Hills, built in 1880 and requisitioned by the Australian Government for use by SOA. They could now talk freely about their achievement and Lyon informed them that Allied intelligence sources had confirmed that the Japanese had no clue as to who had carried out the attack.

Formal picture of the crew of Krait at Meigunyah House

Krait crew have a well-earned celebration at Meigunyah House

The crew had been expecting major headlines in the Australian press about Jaywick's success to both boost flagging morale in Australia and in the free world but, as nothing appeared, they remained sworn to secrecy. By this time, intercepted and decoded Japanese signals had indicated that local Chinese, under the direction of British civilians interned in the Changi Gaol, were responsible for attacking the ships. Consequently, although it was known that the local population was being put through the mill, a decision was made at a high level to keep Jaywick a permanent secret, as other raids of a similar nature might not be able to be carried out.

With Jaywick declared a brilliant success by those in the know, Lyon was invited to dinner by General Blamey, Commander in Chief of Australian Forces. Blamey, the most senior of the Australian generals, had a chequered career, and was certainly not respected by his subordinates. It is said that success has many fathers, but failure is an orphan and it certainly now seemed that way, as Blamey, to whom SOA was answerable, was now trying to cosy up to Lyon, so that he could be associated with Jaywick's success. Lyon, still chaffing over the decisions to keep Jaywick a secret, was disgusted, telling Jaywick's Bettina Reid he would not attend the dinner. 'If I had to sit opposite that man, I would choke,' he said, and sent Page in his place.

Operation Jaywick, led by Ivan Lyon, was the only completely successful mission carried out behind the lines in the South-west Pacific in World War II, achieving its goal without the loss of a single man. However, unbeknown to the elated Jaywick team, a fellow compatriot was heading into mortal danger – Bill Reynolds.

After *Krait*'s engine had self-destructed off the Queensland coast, putting Jaywick on the backburner indefinitely, Bill had left the ship in Cairns and joined the United States Bureau of Economic Warfare, a cover name for the American version of SOE. On 7 November, as the Jaywick team was preparing for its celebration party in Brisbane, Reynolds had left Fremantle in a United States' submarine, USS *Tuna*, captained by Lieutenant Commander J T Hardin. It was his 9th war patrol, and all he had been told was that he was to drop off an agent on an island off Borneo's south-easterly tip.

On the night of 14 November, *Tuna* surfaced just off Laut Island, and Reynolds paddled ashore not far from Sembamban, south-east of Banjarmasin. Although he was 51 years old, it was a solo mission to collect intelligence from Chinese agents operating in the area. Reynolds' cover story was that he was a black marketeer seeking to purchase a junk loaded with rubber and quinine, products essential to both sides in the war effort. Once he had collected his intelligence, he was to sail the junk back to the American base at Exmouth Gulf. It was by all accounts a near suicide mission and highly questionable, but Reynolds considered it was no more risky than any of the activities in which he had participated since Malaya fell to the Japanese.

However, luck was not with him. His presence was betrayed to the Japanese and he was captured at the village of Kota Bahru, where he was held for 8 days, before before being transferred north to Balikpapan. He was imprisoned there in a squalid cell at Sentosa Barracks, which had been converted to a gaol. His Japanese captors were highly suspicious because of his fluency in the Malay language and, after three very long months, he was transferred to Surabaya in Java. He was held there for another six months in solitary confinement until 8 August 1944, when he was dragged out of his cell and loaded onto a truck. He and other prisoners – a mix of Indonesians and Europeans – were driven to a place of execution at the Eastern Fort, on Surabaya's harbour.

The prisoners were to be decapitated. The Japanese traditionally regarded this as death with honour but, when prisoners of war were involved, it often degenerated into a blood bath, with junior military personnel volunteering to act as executioners, simply to see what it was like. The swordsmen, who arrived late, were clearly not experienced in the task and the first batch beheaded suffered an excruciating end. Those who were to be next, having witnessed their fellow prisoners being butchered, were rendered totally incapacitated and quite incapable of kneeling, or sitting on the edge of the pit. The Japanese Commanding Officer then gave orders to shoot the rest, who had collapsed in terror. That left Reynolds, who was to be put to the sword.

The tough, tall Australian, who was head and shoulders above the Japanese, was not about to cooperate by bending or kneeling while someone cut off his head. Realising that the prisoner, who was standing rigidly at attention, was not going to yield, the commanding officer called up a firing squad to do the job.

On 13 November 1946, three years after Reynolds left the submarine on his fateful solo mission, his beloved wife, Bridget, received his MBE from the Duke of Gloucestershire at Government House, Melbourne.

Chapter Twelve

Scapegoat スケープゴート

The attack on Singapore had come as a terrible shock to the Japanese occupying forces. Their arrogance at being impregnable disallowed them to consider that external forces could have been responsible for sinking the ships. Believing it was an inside job, the Japanese secret police or Kempeitai, who had long held suspicions about the activities of Singaporean Chinese, turned their attention on known sympathisers.

The majority of the Chinese in Singapore hated the Japanese, far more than the Malays, who had more placid temperaments and at that time were generally pro-Japanese. The Kempeitai, who were already investigating local Chinese in regard to what they believed were various acts of sabotage, concluded that they too must be responsible for the attack on the shipping. With suspects already in their sights, and with Singapore so deep in their own territory, they never considered that it could have been a seaborne attack.

The Kempeitai Headquarters were in the former YMCA (Young Men's Christian Association) building on Stamford Road, in the middle of town, with an auxiliary torture house on Smith Street, where prisoners were also subjected to daily torture for quite minor misdemeanours. The Kempeitai, in attempting to solve the mystery of the attack, concluded that British internees in Changi Gaol had planned it, and that it had been carried out by subversive Chinese.

On 10 October 1943, two weeks after the Jaywick raid, the Kempeitai – led by Colonel Haruzo Sumida – arrested 57 prisoners in connection with what the Japanese termed the 'Singapore Incident'. Occurring on the tenth day of the tenth month, the arrests and what followed would become known in Singapore as the 'Double Tenth Incident'.

One of the chief suspects for masterminding the attack was Robert Healy Scott, a British barrister who had previously served in Singapore as a senior Foreign Office official, and who was thought by the Japanese to be a troublesome ringleader. Scott himself presumed that the attack must have been carried out by Chinese operatives trained by SOE at 101 Specialist Training School, where Lyon and Morris had worked. Sumida, however, was convinced that Scott and accomplices had planned the sabotage and sinking of the ships from within the prison.

On 11 October, everyone in the gaol, women and children included, were ordered to parade in the prison square, while the Kempeitai carried out a thorough search to find evidence that would substantiate their theory. However, although they found radios, money and diaries, there was nothing that could possibly be related to the attack. Determined to get to the bottom of the matter, they arrested their 'suspects' for questioning, and transferred them to the interrogation centre.

Then followed a long period of terror, as the Kempeitai tried to convince their superiors that they had apprehended those responsible for the Japanese humiliation. The torture houses on Stamford Road and Smith Street worked around the clock, with the screams of the victims clearly audible to passers by. When not undergoing various forms of hideous torture, those under suspicion were crowded into cages, regardless of sex, with no bedding. By day, from 0800 to 2200 hours, they were made to sit on the floor, upright with knees bent, and with their hands not allowed to touch the floor. There was a strict ban on any communication or talking. Any infringement would result in an immediate and severe beating. Some 'confessed', only to retract the confession when released from their agony. As the weeks passed, the Kempeitai had no evidence, just confessions from individuals who had been pushed to breaking point.

The treatment handed out during interrogation included being beaten all over the body with iron bars, brass rods, bamboo sticks, wet knotted ropes, belts with buckles and revolver butts. On most occasions, the beatings were administered while the victim was suspended from a beam by the wrists. One prisoner was flogged more than 200 times in one session, a torture repeated for 4-5 days in a row, with stints of up to 55 hours. One beating, which lasted more than 100 hours, resulted in the prisoner's death.

Others, hands tied behind their backs, were forced to kneel on sharp pieces of wood, with other sharp pieces of wood or metal placed behind their knees so as to cut into the flesh of their calves or thighs as they knelt. To ramp up the degree of pain for what was known as 'the log torture', the interrogators jumped on the prisoner's thighs or on the projecting ends of the bars and wood. Some undergoing this torture had Japanese perch on their shoulders, or were forced to hold heavy weights above their heads, to increase the pressure on their knees, which, in turn, increased damage to the flesh on their legs. Occasionally, they also received blows to the body.

The Kempeitai were expert in keeping victims in a state of semi-consciousness by inflicting insufficient force to have them actually pass out. In what was known as 'the water torture', a cloth was placed over the victim's mouth and nose and water steadily forced down the throat. Once the stomach could hold no more water, the Japanese jumped on it, from a height, forcing the water out. Prisoners, male and female, were routinely burned with cigarettes between their toes, under the armpits and in the most sensitive and intimate parts of their bodies. Several Chinese had petrol poured onto their abdomens and were set on fire, while another had his hands, after being dunked in methylated spirits, set alight.

As time went by, the Kempeitai dreamt up new ways of trying to force a confession, including electrocution, while other victims were informed of their imminent execution, either by decapitation or firing squad, and instructed to write letters to their loved ones. They were then tied to a post or ordered to kneel, with hoods placed over their heads. Expecting death, which in some cases may have been a merciful release, they were instead reprieved, with some victims passing out because the strain was so great. In total, 57 British civilian internees from the gaol were arrested. Twelve did not survive the interrogations. Two others were beheaded. The torture was so severe that one tried to commit suicide by jumping from a high balcony. Although he severely fractured his pelvis, his captors propped him up and continued to torture and interrogate him until he died.

Many Chinese living in Singapore, also believed to be implicated, were tortured and then thrown into Outram Road Gaol, a forbidding 19th century prison condemned for further use by the British. Reopened by the Kempeitai, it became a maximum security punishment facility for Japanese military and Allied POWs, along with civilians, sentenced to terms of imprisonment for violating some law or other. Most of the Chinese were not in Outram Road for long. After 'confessing' under torture they were beheaded and their heads stuck on spikes at street corners in an effort to intimidate the culprits to come forward. None of those tortured and executed had any idea of the crimes for which they had been arrested.

One young woman of Chinese descent came to the attention of the secret police – Elizabeth Choy who, prior to the occupation, had taught at St Andrew's School and served as a second lieutenant in the Singapore Volunteer Corps, where she was fondly known as 'Gunner Choy'. Although deeply religious, Elizabeth had a deep hatred of the Japanese as her brother had been executed, along with tens of thousands of other Chinese, shortly after the occupation of Singapore in what was known as Sook Ching (Operation Cleanup). Any Chinese person who was academic, spoke English, wore Western style clothing or was a person of influence, was ruthlessly killed. Elizabeth and her husband Khun Heng had done well to avoid the same fate.

Surviving the purge, the couple had opened a canteen at Tan Tok Seng Hospital and established a service to ferry civilian internees in makeshift ambulances to and from Singapore's hospitals. On the ambulance runs they were able to deliver letters, fresh clothing, food, and medicine to the internees, as well as to gather information on troop movements and ships coming in and out of Singapore. This intelligence was passed to agents in Singapore who had the means to transmit it to the Allies.

Following a tip-off that the Choys were smuggling money to internees in Changi Gaol, the Kempeitai arrested Elizabeth's husband and subjected him to prolonged interrogation. After a week passed, a fearful Elizabeth went to Kempeitai HQ but, to her disbelief and anguish, they denied all knowledge of her husband's arrest or having him in custody. Three weeks later, with still no knowledge of his whereabouts or condition, Elizabeth was arrested. In her initial interrogation, she was told of the sinking of Japanese ships in the harbour, to which she was allegedly connected, and accused of handling large sums of money, before being stripped naked and repeatedly electrocuted. At one stage her husband, who had been receiving much the same treatment, was brought in and made to watch in the hope of making him crack. Elizabeth resisted the interrogations, remained stoic and admitted nothing. Her husband, having made a false confession after watching his young wife being tortured, was sentenced to imprisonment in Outram Road Gaol for 12 years.

Elizabeth was released after 200 days in captivity and torture, having lost half of her body weight. A total of 143 named Chinese were executed at Outram Road Gaol from May 1943 until the war ended in August 1945. Exactly how many of these were victims of the Double Tenth is not known, neither is it known how many other unnamed Chinese were executed because of Operation Jaywick, but the number of heads on spikes increased in proportion to the arrests. Tragically, the suffering as a result of the raid spread beyond those arrested and tortured. At Changi Gaol, the far from adequate rations issued to the internees were cut further and concerts, school lessons and any forms of entertainment banned.

The Double Tenth Massacre, as it became known, was the terrible price paid by the prisoners and the local community for the success of Operation Jaywick. The reign of terror would last twelve long months and, at the end of that period, the Kempeitai still had no clue as to how the highly effective acts of sabotage had been committed.

On release from prison, Elizabeth Choy might have expected some support and solace after her terrible treatment, but she was given the cold shoulder by much of the population, terrified to be seen talking or helping her. She later told a friend that 'there is nothing more aggravating than calmness.'

After the war, this very brave woman and her husband were invited to recuperate in England, where they remained for four years. During that time they were invited to a private audience with the Queen in St James's Palace, where they were both awarded the Order of the British Empire for assisting British prisoners of war in Singapore during the occupation.

At the war's end, the Japanese who inflicted such terrible suffering and death on their victims faced justice. Twenty-one of the Kempeitai involved were charged with war crimes. Eight received the death sentence, seven were acquitted, and the remainder given prison sentences ranging from one year to life. However, no form of punishment would ever heal the pain and suffering experienced by so many innocent people.

Lyon, aggrieved that the success of Jaywick had not been used to maximum effect as propaganda, bloodying the nose of his arch enemy, was aware that local elements were being blamed, but was unaware of the terrible price being exacted by the ruthless Kempeitai.

SOA however, knew from intercepted wireless signals that the Japanese had instructed ports in their area of occupation to tighten security. Although the state of alert applied throughout the region, the main culprits involved in the attacks on shipping were deemed to be local insurgents, a fact made clear to SOA in decoded intercepts which read 'Singapore shipping espionage is carried out by natives under European instruction. An enemy espionage affair developed early in the morning of 27 September 1943 at Singapore and was commanded by Europeans hiding in the neighbourhood of Pulai in Johore', and, later, 'In Singapore on the morning of 27 September six ships of 2000 to 5000 tons (three tankers among them) were sunk by bombs due to a clever plan by Malays working under the supervision of caucasians directing behind the scenes'.

The decision by SOA's most senior personnel to keep Jaywick a secret was therefore made in full knowledge that local people were being blamed and would most certainly be reaping the retribution of the Japanese. If Jaywick had been used as a propaganda tool, as Lyon had intended, so much suffering could, and would, have been avoided.

However, it didn't seem to bother anyone at SOA. War is a nasty business and the deaths were possibly regarded as collateral damage or the price paid for engaging in warfare. Or maybe the lives of the local population simply didn't matter. The general attitude at that time was that anyone who was not white was expendable. The consequences of Operation Jaywick were not widely known until 1990, and not publicised in the press until 1993, the 50th Anniversary of the mission. Even then, the disclosure that so many inmates of Changi prison and Singaporeans had suffered so horribly as a result of the mission was not received well in some quarters. It was not until 2003, sixty years after the event, that the Australian government finally acknowledged the price paid for Jaywick and laid, for the first time, a wreath in memory of the Double Tenth victims. It was placed alongside another, to honour the men who had sailed on *Krait* to carry out the most daring Allied mission of World War II.

Chapter Thirteen

Aftermath – from Miner to Major

After recovering from the injury to his ankle military records show, my father Ron Morris was recruited from SOA to SOE's Force 136 Headquarters in Kandy, at that time the capital of Ceylon. Following Singapore's fall, the remnants of the Oriental Mission had been absorbed into Force 136, established to encourage and supply resistance movements in Japanese-occupied territory, and to mount clandestine sabotage operations. Two Oriental Mission members, Davis and Broom, who had reached India with Lyon on *Sederhana Djohanes*, also joined Force 136, along with Freddie Spencer Chapman. All three linked up with local guerrilla units, fighting in the jungle of Malaya and committing very effective acts of sabotage. My father never divulged what he did following Jaywick, but his records show he was employed by SOE until the end of the war.

In early 1944, while in Ceylon, my father was informed that he had been recommended for a Military Medal, Lyon a Distinguished Service Order and Page a Military Cross. On learning of the impending announcements and the details of Jaywick, still very much top-secret, Australian Prime Minister John Curtin wrote to the Acting Governor General, recommending that Lyon be awarded the Victoria Cross and seeking an upgrade for Page.

My dear Acting Governor General,

With reference to the communication of Lord Gowrie on 22 May, 1944, advising that the bestowal of the Distinguished Service Order on Major Ivan Lyon, the Military Cross on Lieutenant R.C. Page, and the Military Medal on Corporal A. Crilly and R.G. Morris, have been approved, it will no doubt have come to your Excellency's knowledge that for certain reasons the promulgation of these awards was suspended pending further investigations.

In light of information which has since been made available concerning the operation in which these four persons were engaged, it would appear that recognition of a higher standard would be justified in the first two cases, namely Lyon and Page, and I would be obliged if Your Excellency would kindly seek His Majesty's consent for the cancellation of the Distinguished Service Order and Military Cross approved to these cases.

I consider that the services rendered by Major Ivan Lyon would be more appropriately recognised by the bestowal on him of the Victoria Cross for great valour and devotion to duty in most hazardous undertakings, and that the Distinguished Service Order would be more fitting in Lieutenant Page's case that the services rendered by him were similar and equivalent to those rendered by Lieutenant D.M.N Davidson RNVR, who has already received the Distinguished Service Order on the recommendations of the United Kingdom authorities.

John Curtin

The Australian Prime Minister's recommendation was seconded by Lord Selbourne, who was the UK's Minister for Economic Warfare, with responsibility for SOE operations. Lord Selbourne had met Lyon in SOE HQ in Baker Street, London. Writing to Lyon's grandfather when Lyon, who had embarked on a mission known as Operation Rimau in October 1944 and was reported missing in action, Selbourne stated, "I tried to get your son the V.C. and spoke and wrote several times to General Sir Thomas Blamey about it".

Prime Minister Curtin's letter was forwarded to London and, subsequently, as a result of Curtin's actions, Page was indeed awarded a DSO. However Lyon's VC was turned down by a committee of naval and military personnel. A reply was received from the Governor General, The Secretary of State for Dominion Affairs,

No 12 Secret Honours

Your telegram 24 October. The case of Lyon has been most carefully considered in view of the authorities here including Admiralty, who were consulted as the expedition was undertaken at sea. His action, although an extremely gallant one, did not quite reach the very high standard of outstanding gallantry required for the award of the Victoria Cross. It is accordingly proposed to submit the name to the King for a Distinguished Service Order. The recommendation that an award of the MC to Page be augmented to DSO will also be submitted to His Majesty. It is hoped that action will in the circumstances be agreeable to your Prime Minister.

One theory at the time was that the Admiralty had blocked Lyon's VC. It was thought that to have highlighted a seaborne operation, the deepest ever conducted behind enemy lines and led by an army officer, would not have made the navy look good. At the same time, McDowell the engineer had been awarded a Distinguished Service Medal, with Military Medals going to Crilly the cook and Morris. The disparity was noted by *Krait*'s crew and other naval personnel, who felt, quite rightly, that the army contingent on *Krait* did better out of the honours bestowed. There appear to have been valid reasons for this, which have been examined and recorded by others.

The undeniable success of Jaywick created the desire for SOA to strike back with confidence at the enemy, behind their lines and with far greater capacity. Lyon, who had previously encountered barriers and negativity, was delighted with the positive attitudes now being displayed. General MacArthur had also become very interested and sent an instruction for Lyon to meet with him. *This*, Lyon thought, *was surely the green light to even greater things.*

Thankfully, my father was not recruited to the new operation, Operation Rimau, being planned by SOA off the back of Operation Jaywick, whose success provided fertile ground for Lyon to press home the case for a further and even more devastating attack. Strikes undertaken by special forces were seen as very high value, and doors previously closed were now opened.

Lord Louis Mountbatten, Supreme Allied Commander, was also urging SOA to commit to further raids against the Japanese. The British and Australians were aware that, in the final stages of the war, they could not match the logistics and manpower of the Americans, required to win the war in the Pacific.

Tragically, all 23 men assigned to Operation Rimau, including Lyon, Davidson, Page, Falls, Huston and Marsh, lost their lives. Lyon and Huston were killed in action and Davidson used his cyanide capsule to avoid inevitable capture. Marsh died in captivity from illness. Page, Falls and eight others, after being confined in Outram Road Gaol, were taken to wasteland off Reformatory Road (now Clementi) where they were beheaded on 7 July 1945, five weeks before the war ended.

On cessation of hostilities, my father was returned to his parent regiment, the RAMC. Back on normal regimental duties, he married and started a family, at the same time maintaining his military career.

However, this relative normality did not last for long. In 1949 he was posted to Malaya as part of Operation Far East Land Forces (FARELF), as the British High Command was deeply concerned that they had the responsibility of holding back Communist insurgency in Malaya with a massively depleted military force. The detail of my father's involvement is unknown to me. All I can remember is, as a young boy, he explained to me something called 'winning hearts and minds', which I now know was the

British strategy at that time – to engage and win over the indigenous population. This successful military intervention effectively ensured that Malaya and Singapore would become flourishing democracies and economies.

In February 1965, Dad was sent to Borneo on active service during the Konfrontasi (1963-1966), when the Indonesians tried to take over the British territories of Sarawak and British North Borneo, now known as Sabah. As Adjutant to 19 Field Ambulance, RAMC, he was responsible for setting up emergency medical facilities in the jungle. On his return to the UK, the Malaysian Government made a request for a suitably qualified British officer to coordinate and help the Malaysian Army establish and train the first Malaysian Field Ambulance. Dad was selected for this task, primarily because of his knowledge of that part of the world and its culture, and his natural empathy with its people. This time however, he was able to take his wife and two children with him to his posting in Kuala Lumpur based at an old British military hospital in Kinrara. Retiring from the British Army in 1972 with the rank of major, he and my mother Pat moved to his beloved Wales, where my mother died in 1996, followed three years later by my father.

His coffin, draped with the Union Jack, was a silent but poignant reminder of a lifetime of serving the nation, of devotion to duty, of putting the welfare of others before himself. The bugle played the Last Post and his Regimental colours bearing the motto 'In Ardus Fidelis' were lowered to honour Taffy Morris who had gone on to lead a long and fulfilling life, facing and overcoming many other dangers along the way, as he worked his way steadily and without fuss through the ranks. From Miner to Major - a fitting epitaph.

My father's life was shaped by his war experiences as he had achieved the almost impossible by joining the army prior to the war as a private soldier and rising up through the ranks to become a major. Something quite incredible for an ex-miner from the Rhonda. In the following years and throughout his career he never forgot the loss of his wartime colleagues, especially Ivan Lyon.

It took quite some time before Jaywick was made public. Although Operation Rimau and the beheading of ten of its members was reported in the press on 2 November 1945, it was not for another nine days, on Remembrance Day, that anyone learned of Operation Jaywick and its success. Other stories followed but there was no official acknowledgement of the raid until 1 August 1946, nine months later, when Francis Ford, the Australian Minister for the Army, made a statement in the Australian House of Representatives.

'The story of a well-kept secret has now been released with the publication of the awards for gallantry to a small but determined band of officers and men who carried the war thousands of miles behind the Japanese lines during the days of 1943, when Japan was flushed with the fortunes of conquest. The exploit was a joint effort by a party of 14, comprising of ten Australians and four members of the British Forces. Unfortunately, six members lost their lives in a subsequent operation in 1944. The awards were approved by the King in 1944, but details were withheld for security reasons. I give now the names and awards, and also the home states of the Australians,

British Army. Captain (Later Lieutenant-Colonel) Ivan Lyon, M.B.E, D.S.O, Gordon Highlanders.

Royal Navy. Lieutenant (Later Lieutenant Commander) Donald Davidson, D.S.O, Royal Naval Reserve.

New South Wales. Lieutenant (Later Captain) Page D.S.O, Australian Imperial Forces.

New South Wales. Lieutenant Hubert Carse, M.I.D, Royal Australian Naval Volunteer Reserve.

Royal Navy. Leading Stocker James McDowell, D.S.M.

New South Wales. Leading Telegraphist Horace Young, M.I.D, Royal Australian Navy.

Queensland. Corporal Andrew Crilly, M.M, Australian Imperial Force.

British Army. Corporal Ronald Morris, MM, BEM, Royal Army Medical Corps.

Queensland. Acting Leading Seaman Kevin Cain, M.I.D, Royal Australian Navy.

Western Australia. Able Seaman Arthur Jones, D.S.M, Royal Australian Navy.

South Australia. Acting Able Seaman Mostyn Berryman, M.I.D, Royal Australian Navy.

New South Wales. Acting Able Seaman Walter Falls, D.S.M, Royal Australian Navy. (Life lost in subsequent operation in 1944.)

Queensland. Acting Able Seaman Andrew Huston D.S.M, Royal Australian Navy. (Life lost in subsequent operation in 1944.)

Queensland. Acting Able Seaman Frederick Marsh, M.I.D, Royal Australian Navy.

I am sure that all Honourable Members will join with me in expressing admiration for the heroic deeds and gallant men. Our hearts go out in sympathy to the relatives of those who subsequently lost their lives.

It was by such deeds that the Allies won the war.'

Bibliography

Brook, Geoffrey, *Singapore's Dunkirk*, 1989

Connell, Brian, *Return of the Tiger*, 1960

Gough, Richard SOE Singapore 1941- 42, 1985

Gough, Richard, *The Escape from Singapore*, 1987

Handwritten log book of MV *Krait* on Operation Jaywick. (Quotations from the log in The Tiger's Revenge are verbatim from the official original document)

McKie, Ronald, *The Heroes*, 1960

Davidson, Donald Camp X Log

Morris, Ronald George, 7264507, SOE Records, UK National Archives, Kew

Morris, Ronald George, 7264507, Military Records Office, Glasgow

Silver, Lynette Ramsay, *Deadly Secrets*, 2010

Silver, Lynette Ramsay, *The Heroes of Rimau*, 1990

Thompson, Julian *War Behind Enemy Lines*, 1988

Thompson, Peter and Macklin, Robert, *Kill Tiger*, 2002

Thompson, Peter, *The Battle for Singapore*, 2005

Wynyard, Noel, *Winning Hazard*, 1948

The End

Milton Keynes UK
Ingram Content Group UK Ltd.
UKHW040944051023
430000UK00004B/233